Photograph by Jane Miller

Contents

Crystal Clear 6
by Carol Vaughan
Illustrated by Sally Bell

Limericks 13

Pony Club Horse Trials Championships 14

Readers' Poems 17

International Mounted Games Visit 18
by Suzanne Charlton

Readers' Quiz 20

Pony Club Show Jumping 21

Many Moods 22
Photographs by Sally Anne Thompson

Dressage Has Its Uses 26
by Domini Lawrence

Fair Exchange 28
by Deborah Ghate
Illustrated by Carolyn Dinan

Buying a Pony 35
by Simone French

Crossword Puzzle 38

Pony Club Polo 39
by Cynthia Muir

Pony Club Mounted Games 43

Riders of Renown 44

More Moods 56
Photographs by Jane Miller

Fergus 59
by Denise Amos
Illustrated by Elaine Roberts

How to Draw Horses 64
by Christine Bousfield

Into Novice One-day Events 66
by Anna Buxton

Competition 72

Pony Club Polo Tournament 74

Readers' Poems 76

Answers to Puzzles

1979 Competition Results 77

SBN 361 04570 0
Copyright © 1979 Purnell and Sons Limited
Published 1979 by Purnell Books,
Berkshire House, Queen Street,
Maidenhead, Berkshire
Made and printed in Great Britain by
Purnell and Sons Limited,
Paulton (Bristol) and London

The Pony Club
Annual

Edited by
Genevieve Murphy

Purnell

Crystal Clear

by Carol Vaughan

Illustrated by Sally Bell

In the school train Crystal Morrison sat by the window, lost in her thoughts, unaware of the excited clamour all about her. Her mother would be meeting her in London, to drive down to the new house in the country, the first time that they had had a real home in England. And there was stabling. For two. A bit ramshackle, but it had been done up, along with the house, by a local carpenter, and all it needed was a coat of whitewash, some spit and polish ... And her mother had written to say that they had heard of a likely pony for her, a promising jumper, through new friends.

In her mind's eye, Crystal saw the pony ... her pony ... a rich bay, galloping alongside the train, flying the hedges as they clickety-clicked past, steadying for a massive gate, striding out to clear a shallow stream meandering across a meadow, baulking at a steep bank down onto a busy road, as the train thundered over a bridge ... but the suburban houses broke into her daydream and she came back to reality, to the chattering girls all around her, to the wheezing gasp of braking wheels.

Miranda Vallon lugged her suitcase off the rack, almost dropping it on Crystal's head. "Wake up, dreamy," she said. "We're nearly there. Thinking about your pony, I suppose. As we are going to be neighbours, I hope you get something good, then you can ride with me. See you at the Pony Club meeting on Thursday. Mr Boots has been away, being schooled, ready for me to jump him this summer, but he came back yesterday."

*   *   *

The house stood back from the road, behind a rather untidy lawn, low and warm in weathered red brick with a dark roof, the new paintwork gleaming. An old man was stooping over the flowerbed bordering the house.

"That's Larry," said Mrs Morrison. "Isn't it lucky? He's just retired here, to live with a married daughter, after his wife died; he worked here when he was a boy, sixty years ago, and he comes three or four mornings a week, depending on his rheumatism. They call him 'Loopy Larry' in the village, but he seems quite normal to me. He's a dear old man."

"And this afternoon we are going to see the pony," insisted Crystal, little interested in Larry, or the garden for that matter.

"Yes," said Mrs Morrison, smiling. "I do hope you'll like him. Daddy met a man, Mr Barking, and he said he had a friend, Ted Barrett, who ran a stables and would be sure to be able to fix you up. And, sure enough, Mr Barrett said he had just the pony for you when Daddy telephoned. We told him how keen you were and how well you got on at school and at the places where you have been on riding holidays while we were abroad so much, and that you wanted to go in for jumping. And now that Daddy is settled in England, except for short trips like this one, and you'll be able to be a day girl next term . . . everything seems to be working out wonderfully." Mrs Morrison had always felt guilty about farming her daughter out on relations and at holiday homes while she had been obliged to travel so much with her husband, but now she would be able to make up for all that.

*   *   *

Selsdon Glory came out of the stable with a bounce, neck stiffly arched, eyes rolling, fighting the hand on his reins. Crystal and Mrs Morrison stepped back as the pony pranced towards the jumping field where Glynis, the stable girl,

swung lightly into the saddle, curbing his exuberance with a practised hand.

"Goes a treat, don't he?" said Ted Barrett, tapping his booted leg with a stick. "Of course, he's not a novice ride, but you don't want some old slowcoach, do you? Go right to the top in the right hands, that pony will. If I wasn't so overstocked, with this new Irish consignment . . ." he let the sentence trail away into the air, with practised ease—he had been using it for years to trap gullible buyers!

Glynis took the pony over the six permanent fences in the field, Crystal glorying in the free-striding enthusiasm with which the pony swept through the brush fence and over the wall—and he was a rich bay, just like her dream pony!

"Well, what do you say?" asked Ted, briskly.

"Well, I don't know . . ." began Mrs Morrison, flustered. "Perhaps Crystal . . . shouldn't you try him?"

Mr Barrett glanced at his watch. "Time for a quick one," he said, with a guffaw. "Here, Glynis. Put the lady up. Just the pony for her, eh, Glynis?"

Glynis dismounted with a tired air and Crystal, almost shaking with excitement, tried the leathers for length, mounted, while Ted stood to the pony's head and Glynis held down the off stirrup, and settled herself in the saddle. Selsdon Glory felt very bouncy after the riding school ponies she had ridden—but none of them had been potential champion show jumpers, Crystal reminded herself.

"Once round the field and over the brush fence," bawled Ted Barrett, as she rode off.

It did not take long to go round the field, the pony's neck strained in front of her against the pull of the standing martingale, his ears pricked until they almost met in

the middle. Crystal took him over the jump, sitting as well as she could, but was still almost left behind by the enormous, plunging leap with which the pony cleared the fence. Her cheeks pink with excitement—and pain, because she had bitten her tongue—she rode back to the three spectators, Glynis taking the pony's head as she dismounted.

Mrs Morrison was faintly embarrassed by the obvious enthusiasm on Crystal's face. One should bargain with dealers, point out faults, she felt, not quite knowing how to begin.

"That pony's worth every penny of £500," said Ted Barrett.

"£500?" squeaked Mrs Morrison. "But you said £350 when my husband telephoned you last week, before he went abroad."

Ted Barrett clapped the stick against his leg with a resounding noise which made the pony jump away nervously. "*Now* I remember!" he exclaimed. "That was before Glory jumped at . . . Ah,

well, Ted Barrett's a man of his word," he said resignedly. Sorrowfully he shook his head—Glynis repressed a grin, she had seen his 'act' so often and it seldom failed—"£350 and here's my hand on it." Ted Barrett grasped Mrs Morrison's reluctant hand with a horny clasp.

"Th . . . thank you," said Mrs Morrison, flustered. "And now . . . . perhaps I can give you a cheque?"

"Certainly, Madam," said Ted Barrett, beaming. "Step right into my office. Put the pony away, Glynis. I have a van going your way tomorrow, I can drop him off, tack and all—that's a bit extra, of course. And the vet's certificate." He pursed his lips, sighing. They hadn't even asked if the pony was warranted sound . . . but Selsdon Glory was sound, so he hadn't needed to think up a tale about that.

Crystal followed the pony worshipfully into the stable as Glynis led him in, whistling through the straw clenched between her teeth, avoiding Crystal's eye. She had seen so many young hopefuls come bouncing in and leave, with their hearts high and some totally unsuitable pony . . . if Ted hadn't given her ten quid every time she helped him unload a dud . . .

*   *   *

Selsdon Glory arrived the next morning. The driver let down the ramp and brought the snorting pony out with a rush. Selsdon Glory stood looking round distrustfully as Crystal clung to the halter rope and gazed at him adoringly. Old Larry, leaning on a fork, watched them put the pony into the loosebox where he whirled round, clattering on the hard floor with shod hooves, colliding with the door as he stuck his head out to look at his new home.

Crystal arranged her tack neatly

"Isn't he super, Larry?"

in the harness room, hardly able to wait till the afternoon when there was a Pony Club meeting where she would be able to show off her new pony and meet other local riders—besides the insufferable Miranda Vallon, always swanking about her top show jumper, Mr Boots.

"Isn't he super, Larry?" she called happily to the old gardener. "He's just like my dream pony, the one I've always wanted."

Larry smiled at her, old eyes twinkling in his wrinkled face. "Nice looking pony," he said. "I wish you luck with him."

The Pony Club meeting was held at the home of Colonel Charters, five miles from Crystal's house.

Crystal hacked over, allowing plenty of time, and arrived first, finding it difficult to control the hotted up pony who danced and pulled and lathered himself into a muck sweat, just hacking along a quiet country road. Crystal was exhausted, her hands pink and sore, her legs aching, when she arrived.

The Colonel's groom, Weston, showed her where she could tether the pony, in a nearby field. "Better walk him round, till the others arrive," he advised. "Cool him off; never was a pony like Glory for making a fuss about nothing."

"Do you know him, then?" asked Crystal, surprised.

Weston grinned wryly. "Know

him? You're the third mu . . . the third girl who's come to Pony Club meetings on Glory. Ted Barrett should've called him Boomerang; he always gets him back. Too hot for a child and too small for an adult, Glory is."

"But I bought him as a jumper," cried Crystal, aghast.

"Oh, sure, he can jump—if he happens to be facing in the right direction when he reaches the fence," said Weston. "Ted's got him schooled over those six fences until he daren't put a foot wrong, but you try `him outside, and it's another story."

Crystal attended the lecture full of foreboding about her new pony, which was not lessened during the riding session afterwards, when Selsdon Glory barged, shied, bumped and plunged, amongst the ponies, fighting his bit, wild-eyed, until he was lathered to the ears. Three times he had her off, swerving unexpectedly and bolting off across the field, while Miranda Vallon watched superciliously from Mr Boots' well-schooled back.

"Oh, really, Crystal," she cried, "couldn't you have bought something a bit more manageable? No one can ride that stupid animal; and you're not going out with me on him. He might kick Mr Boots and lame him for the whole season, and that would be a tragedy."

"I'm going to ride him if it kills me," said Crystal, through clenched teeth. "Thank you," she added, to Bill Benham, another member, who was holding Glory's head for her to mount again—that was another thing she had discovered; no one had ever taught Glory to stand to be mounted.

By the time she reached home again, Crystal was hot, flustered and aching in every limb, but she was not beaten yet. Riding through the village, the pony still stargazing, fighting his bit, she saw old

Larry leaning on his garden wall, gazing at her.

"Had a good ride?" he asked.

"Awful," said Crystal, not mincing matters. "But I'm going to win if I have to rebreak him from the beginning. I'm sure he's a good pony—underneath."

Larry nodded his head wisely. "Too full of himself," he said. "Better if he lived out. Work off some of his energy, that way."

Crystal thought that was a good idea, until she tried to catch Selsdon Glory the next morning. Mrs Morrison kept calling her in to breakfast, until at last she had to give up and go in, to eat congealed bacon and egg.

Old Larry was pottering round the garden when she went out again, wondering desperately what to do as she picked up the halter and bucket. He looked so sympathetic that she told him her troubles.

He nodded understandingly. "Can be difficult," he agreed. "But you can't let him get away with it. If a horse wins one battle, you've

"Had a good ride?"

9

lost them all. Reckon I've read, somewhere, of a man walking a horse down, till he's too tired to go on running away. Do that once and maybe he'll give up. Hey," he added, as Crystal started thoughtfully towards the field, "maybe you'd better ask your Ma for a sandwich; it's lunch-time in only four hours!"

It was three o'clock in the afternoon before Crystal caught Selsdon Glory. After a handful of nuts she turned him loose again. It was past five the next time she caught him, but after that she could walk up to him as she liked, giving him a handful of nuts each time, until he was waiting hopefully for her, even taking a step towards her. Crystal wondered if he was as tired as she was. His ears looked puzzled.

"Maybe he'll give up"

The next morning she took the precaution of breakfasting first, but when she went and rattled the bucket, the pony came without much difficulty and she led him into the stable. He nipped her twice while she was reaching for the girth, until she tied him up tight by the head. Larry came to watch her mounting, as Selsdon Glory swung round in the yard, his hooves beating a rapid tattoo on the cobbles. Larry pulled out a large spotted handkerchief and waved it above his head. Astonished, the pony stopped to stare and Crystal struggled into the saddle. Larry set the pony's forelock straight and ran an enquiring hand down his face, to the bit. Selsdon Glory flung his head up, straining against the standing martingale.

"I have heard that some ponies have very tender mouths," said Larry thoughtfully. "They go better in an ordinary snaffle. Maybe . . . bless me, look at the time; your Ma'll be after me, if she sees me slacking like this!"

Crystal rode out apprehensively; perhaps Selsdon Glory was not quite as difficult as he had been the first time—he must have been tired after his long walk the previous day—but no one could have called him a comfortable ride; his neck was strained too high, making his paces jerky and rough. She didn't stay out for long; she wanted to talk her mother into buying a snaffle, to replace Ted Barrett's contraption.

Mrs Morrison, finding herself the target of other pony mums' scorn at having been taken in by Ted Barrett, with his unmanageable pony, sighed, but bought the snaffle, hoping she wasn't throwing good money after bad.

Crystal, preparing to mount Glory in his new bit for the first time, wished that someone had invented a padded rubber suit, specially for crashing to the ground. Selsdon Glory was difficult enough to hold beforehand. But Larry had been busy, building a makeshift fence between the back of the stable and the outhouse, making a rough, enclosed circle, almost a corral.

He waved her in, shut the gap and leant on his improvised fence, talking almost conversationally, making her turn, stop, start, back, using her weight to guide the pony. Larry wouldn't let her ride him outside, but took her into the field with a lungeing rein, and made her ride without reins or stirrups, sitting, arms folded, while he directed the pony, keeping the long rein always at the right tautness, flicking the long whip with an unexpected skill.

Larry took her into the field with a lungeing rein

quieten the pony down and then let her go out. Selsdon Glory was learning to relax his jaw and he was going more easily, the wild look leaving his eyes; he was still good for a nip in the stable but, it seemed to Crystal, even that was rather half-hearted, more a tiresome habit than an incurable vice.

Several times she went to gymkhanas and local shows, where Miranda was sweeping the board as usual, but she went on foot. Larry wouldn't hear of her taking Selsdon Glory.

"If you start galloping him about before he's ready, you'll be right back where you started," he said sternly.

They were jumping now, in the paddock, all sorts of obstacles thought up—and built—by Larry, but at the first sign of the pony taking command it was back to the cavalletti and, slowly, pony—and rider—improved. Crystal, who had thought that she could ride, knew now that all her knowledge could have been hidden under a horseshoe nail, compared with Larry's bottomless fund of wisdom.

"We'll bring him out in September, at the Pony Club Trials," decided Larry, who had become

If Selsdon Glory was surprised to find himself back at school, Crystal was even more astonished by the teacher. "But where did you learn all this, Larry?" she asked, finding the pony unexpectedly easy to sit as he lolloped obediently round the hunched, shrivelled old man.

Larry smiled. "Helped with horses now and again, I have; when you've lived as long as I have, you've done a bit of everything. And when I was born there were more horses than cars on the roads."

It was days before Larry was satisfied and let her start jumping, and then it was cavalletti, cavalletti and more cavalletti. First on the same circle . . . as Larry said, "If he rushes his jumps, all he can do is go so fast he'll catch up with himself; he'll soon get sick of rush-

ing, when he finds he's not getting anywhere."

After a week or so Larry gave her half an hour in the 'school' to

He was still good for a nip

11

quite proprietorial about both pony and rider, and spent far more than three mornings a week at the Morrisons. "Not too exciting for him, nice natural fences, he should do that easily, now that you have him going properly. And, once you've shown him what you want, who knows where you'll end?"

"But we've wasted a whole summer," said Crystal.

Old Larry shook his head reprovingly. "No time's wasted when you're teaching a horse to give the best of himself," he said severely.

*　　*　　*

On the morning of the Pony Club trials Crystal groomed Selsdon Glory until he shone like a conker; the tack had kept her up till ten the previous evening and been left festooning the kitchen, in case a speck of dust fell on it. When Crystal swung up into the saddle, Selsdon Glory, standing fair and square, arched his neck and snorted, his eyes quiet now, his ears attentive.

Crystal hacked to the course, on Colonel Charters' estate, almost on a loose rein, maintaining a light contact with Selsdon Glory's mouth.

Miranda Vallon was already there, Mr Boots still in his horsebox, when Crystal rode in. Several riders stopped to stare.

"Where *did* you get him?" cried Miranda. "He's the spitting image of Selsdon Glory."

"He *is* Selsdon Glory," said Crystal, smiling happily.

"He looks marvellous," said Bill Benham, admiringly. "How did you do it? Wave a magic wand over him or give him tranquillizers?"

"You're to ride tenth," said Miranda. "I'm right after you. They start in ten minutes. I'd better fetch Boots. I think he's gone off jumping; it bores him now. I'll have to get a better pony next season."

The course, stretching out across the sunlit countryside, was green and inviting. Excited ponies were dashing about between the spectators. Long-suffering mothers were holding ponies, or sandwiches or tack—or all three.

Crystal watched the first riders as, one after the other, they cantered off from the start and over the first brush fence and on across the field to the open ditch. It didn't look difficult, nothing that Selsdon Glory couldn't do—if he didn't hot

"He *is* Selsdon Glory"

up. She couldn't help feeling nervous, but she fought down the sensation, determined not to infect the pony with her doubts. He felt tense between her knees, but he was watching the other ponies with pricked ears, standing quite still.

It was her turn. Crystal rode down to the start, catching Colonel Charters' astonished eye, and was off at the drop of the flag, taking the first fence steadily, determined not to let the pony rush, determined to get round, even slowly, rather than have the slightest upset at the fences. Selsdon Glory strode down the hill, his hooves thudding solidly, rhythmically on the turf, his ears pricked and, suddenly, it was like the train again, only this time it was real, she was on her rich bay pony going across country, perfectly in control, fence after fence flashing beneath her, and she knew that he was enjoying it as much as she was.

"You did a clear round, and in the time limit, how marvellous, darling," babbled her mother, who was standing beside Colonel Charters, near the finish.

"Never seen such a change in a pony," roared Colonel Charters. "How did you do it?"

Crystal grinned. "It took ages and I could never have done it without Larry. It was all him. He always knew what to do next."

"But you were the one who was riding the pony," said Mrs Morrison. "That counts for something, doesn't it, Colonel? It wasn't only old Loopy Larry."

"Loopy Larry!" cried the Colonel. "You mean you know him?"

"He works in the garden for us," said Mrs Morrison, surprised. "He came back to the village to live with a married daughter, when his wife died. Why, do you know him?"

"Loopy Larry!" cried the Colonel. "Is he back again? I must come over for a chat. Best horseman in the county, he was. Worked in the West, as a cowboy, as a young man, I believe. When I was a boy, he was my hero. Had a Music Hall turn, he did, back in the days when there were music halls. The Man with the Looping Lariat, they called him—that's how he was nicknamed Loopy Larry. Did all sorts of tricks with a lariat and a performing horse called Prairie Joe. Trained that horse to do everything except the washing up, his wife used to say. And Larry said he'd have taught it to do that, too, if only there'd been an oat-flavoured washing-up powder. Said Joe didn't like the taste of soap! And then, when Prairie Joe died, a very old horse, Larry wouldn't work with another horse; made a new life for himself, selling garden tools, I think.

"No wonder Selsdon Glory's going like a park hack. Little devil met his match this time—and that's not saying you didn't do a splendid job too, young Crystal, getting him round so well your first time out with him. But, if Loopy Larry's your trainer, that clears up the mystery," chortled the Colonel. "You might say it makes it all crystal clear!"

Limericks

The following are some of the many excellent limericks sent in for the 1979 Competition. Consolation postal orders for £1 have been sent to the non-prizewinners whose limericks are published.

A rider who lived in South Kent,
Had a pony who seemed overbent.
  She cured this evasion,
  With lots of persuasion,
And by singing wherever they went.
(Christine Pattle, 15)

A rider who lived in South Kent,
Over the Channel was sent.
  Her pony said "Neigh,
  I don't like the hay,
And I can't speak the language in Ghent."
(Jane Sawtell, 15)

A rider who lived in South Kent,
Won rosettes wherever she went.
  Her sister from Woking,
  Said "This is provoking,
The judges must surely be bent."
(Sally McNaughton, 11)

A rider who lived in South Kent,
Bought a field that he once had to rent.
  His horse said, "That's potty,
  For the grass there is grotty,"
So he lived on the lawn in a tent!
(Sarah E. Turner, 12)

A rider who lived in South Kent,
Had a pony whose nose was all bent.
  One day we suppose,
  It followed its nose,
And no one yet knows where it went.
(Teresa Starling, 11)

A rider who lived in South Kent,
Was a bit of a dare devil gent.
  He rode at full tilt,
  Clad in only a kilt,
At the Badminton three-day event.
(Carol Cooper, 13)

A rider who lived in South Kent,
Entered a German event.
  When he saw Schockemohle,
  He took off his bowler,
And said "You go first, you're a gent!"
(Claire Oddy, 13)

Pony Club Horse Trials Championships

Richard Hawker (15) and Quaise, members of the Bicester and Warden Hill branch, leaving the Domecq Sherry Garden over the "Weaver's Seat". Richard was "Best Boy" in Section C of the Junior Individual in which he finished sixth

Joanna Croome-Carroll (14) and Terry, members of the Tipperary branch from Ireland, won Section A of the Junior Individual. They are pictured over fence 19, which could be (and was) taken many different ways. Joanna is shown taking the "V" part and aiming at the angled rail, which enabled her to take the shortest route round the clump of trees to the last fence

14

Photographs by Cyril Diamond

Below
Amanda Bond (15) and Mr Teal, members of the Crawley and Horsham branch, won Section C of the Junior Individual. They are pictured over the last fence—the "Open Water"

Above
Joanna Wales (13) and Tulira Maria, the second member of the winning West Norfolk team, at fence 19. Joanna was also second in Section A of the Junior Individual

Below left
Virginia Strawson (15) and Charlie Fox entering the Domecq Sherry Garden by the "Hunting Gate". They were first in Section B of the Junior Individual and also members of the Brocklesby Hunt team which finished second

Below
Brigit Ensten (17) and Carbrooke Charles won Section D of the Junior Individual and were members of the winning West Norfolk team

Readers' Poems

The Show
by Anne Moloney

The creaking of leather, the clanking of bits,
The buckle adjusted to make sure it fits.
The hooves finely polished, the plaits double checked,
The highly-bred ponies are nervous and flecked
With white foam as they wait for their class,
With elegant features and limbs like cut glass.

The heavyweight hunters and brewers with drays,
Assortment of colours, from jet black to greys.
Hamburgers, ice-cream, haynets and oats,
The well assured owner who stands by and gloats
As his valuable pony comes out with first prize,
While spectators crowd round and express their surprise.

Then follows the jumping and gymkhana event,
Last minute entries at the Secretary's tent.
The well-bred J.A's are looking their best,
Oxers and doubles are cleared with fine zest,
And then comes the jump-off to determine first place,
Twelve faults and a roan comes out in disgrace.

And when all is finished comes the winner's parade,
In the main ring, a great cavalcade.
Then show day is over, and ponies are tired,
The hunters and jumpers, the ones that were hired,
Have left from the showground and all gone away,
To a deep bed of straw and a full net of hay.

Calypso
by Susan Diane Murphy

Calypso is my pony's name,
His colour is dark bay,
I rush down to the stables
To see him every day.

He loves to eat, he loves to drink,
He loves to run and roll,
He's seven years of age,
And he's as nippy as a foal.

He's courageous, brave and very bold,
He's quick in every limb,
I love him dearly with all my heart,
I'll never part with him.

International Mounted Games Visit

by Suzanne Charlton

Our tour started in Calgary, in the heart of Canada's "Cowboy Land", world famous for its rodeo. It was here that we gained our first impressions of the good Canadian ponies and met the riders who would represent Canada and the United States in the fifth International Mounted Games Competition. The five of us representing the United Kingdom team were Emma Freeman (Enfield Chace), Susie Furnell (H.H.), Emma Hardy (Woodland), Stephen Price (Banwen) and myself (Cheshire North). Mrs Carmen James (Woodland) was our coach and chaperone.

All the teams were presented with the white stetsons of this area of Alberta, which were continuously being lost but which looked absolutely fabulous when we all went on trail rides! We toured the beautiful city of Calgary and saw the fantastic "Spruce Meadows", the show jumping, dressage and breeding complex in Banff National Park where many large international horse shows are staged.

The teams were split up into groups and billeted on local Pony Club families so that we were all given an insight into the Canadian way of life. The Canadian families (and the Americans with whom we stayed later) were wonderfully hospitable and only too glad to help in any way they could.

From Calgary we travelled north to the town of Red Deer, where we participated in a canoeing expedition and spent the day in Canada's great outdoors, covering nearly thirty miles by canoe with only a few thrills and spills! Then on to Edmonton, where we watched part of the Commonwealth Games and only just missed seeing the Queen, and from there to the British Columbia holiday resort of Kelowna which is deep in the heart of the Rockies. We had a restful day recuperating from the hectic travelling of the previous week before flying to Vancouver, where we were greeted by Holly Gordon, one of the trip's chief organisers and hardest workers. There we were entertained with barbecues and beach parties, taken to see numerous museums as well as Vancouver Island and lovely Stanley Park, treated to two delicious Chinese dinners and given a trip up the Grouse Mountain Sky Ride, which was an experience never to be forgotten, and a terrible ordeal for some! We also travelled down to Seattle in the United States to spend a few days with the Pony Clubs there.

For the rest of our trip we stayed at a log cabin camp at Capilano, a few miles from the centre of Vancouver, near to the famous Capilano Suspension Bridge. Here we met some of our friends from Alberta who had come to compete in the Western Canadian Finals, their equivalent to our Prince Philip Cup Finals at Wembley. The best ponies in the Vancouver area had been pooled into as near equal teams as possible, so that nobody had an unfair advantage, and this system seemed to work very well.

When the draw for the International Mounted Games was announced, we found we would be riding the team of ponies that had finished third of the four teams in the Western Finals. We were not too dismayed by this as we had a practice that evening and all went well.

The weather had deteriorated towards the weekend and the Western Finals had been held indoors at the Southlands Riding Centre, but as our competition was to be televised we were to ride outside in the large outdoor peat arena. When the big day finally dawned we were pleased to see that the weather had brightened up a little. First there was a Grand Parade in front of the cameras led by our coach, Carmen James, proudly holding up our Union Jack which we had brought with us all the way from home.

Things did not go too well for us at the beginning. Our best pony, Goblin, turned sour and refused to do any of the games but Stephen Price, from Wales, swopped on to the spare pony and we gradually managed to close the gap on the Canadians who were in the lead. By the end of the fifteen races everyone was confused and nobody seemed to know who had won, until it was announced that we had tied with the Canadians. So we had a tie-breaker, in which the home team did not go well, and we won by a comfortable margin to keep the United Kingdom's unbeaten record intact.

We were then rushed off for an interview and later presented with our rosettes and medals. The team also received a trophy to commemorate the bicentennial of Captain Cook in British Columbia.

Our train journey back through the Rocky Mountains was something that nobody will ever forget. Those last few days were very sad as we had to say goodbye to our new-found friends, but we promised to have a reunion with them ten years later. We will never forget the great hospitality shown to us by our Canadian and American hosts.

The British team. Left to right: Stephen Price, Susie Furnell, Emma Hardy, Mrs Carmen James (coach and chaperone), Emma Freeman and Suzanne Charlton

Readers' Quiz

Compiled from questions submitted by Claire and Sandra Bellham, Katie Granger and Elaine Marriott

Answers on page 76

1. Is **BAY RUM**
   (a) Red Rum's full sister,
   (b) Winner of the Ladies' National Championship when ridden by Sally Horner or
   (c) a three-day eventer who represented America in Kentucky?

2. Is **LIZ EDGAR**
   (a) David Broome's sister,
   (b) Malcolm Pyrah's cousin or
   (c) Graham Fletcher's sister?

3. Is a **BASUTO**
   (a) a famous make of jumping saddle,
   (b) a breed of pony from Africa or
   (c) the Roman name for a snaffle?

4. Is an **AMERICAN SADDLE HORSE**
   (a) a type of very ornate saddle rack,
   (b) an American breed of horse or
   (c) a term given to strong, powerful horses capable of carrying a heavy stock saddle for long distances?

5. Is the current **WORLD SHOW JUMPING CHAMPION**
   (a) Nelson Pessoa,
   (b) Eddie Macken or
   (c) Gerd Wiltfang?

6. When a horse is said to have a **EWE NECK** does it mean
   (a) the horse has thick hair resembling wool on the underside of the neck,
   (b) it has a very prominent crest or
   (c) the line of the neck from ears to withers is concave?

7. Was **PELE** renamed
   (a) Oatfield Hills,
   (b) Kerrygold or
   (c) Easter Parade?

8. Is a **COFFIN HEAD**
   (a) coarse and ugly,
   (b) very elegant or
   (c) found only in Arabs?

9. Are the **WORLD DRESSAGE CHAMPIONSHIPS** held every
   (a) 2 years,
   (b) 3 years or
   (c) 4 years?

10. Is a **SCORRIER**
    (a) the horse who scores the best marks in a three-day event,
    (b) a bit or
    (c) the man in charge of the digital timing and scoreboard at a major show?

11. Is a **CAYUSE**
    (a) an Indian pony,
    (b) a French horse illness or
    (c) a foreign word for rug?

12. Are **WINDGALLS** usually found on
    (a) the horse's neck,
    (b) the leg or
    (c) the back?

13. Is **CHARLEY** another name for
    (a) a fox,
    (b) a hare or
    (c) the hound that is in front of all the others?

14. Was the **SPORTS PERSONALITY OF THE YEAR** won by
    (a) Prince Charles,
    (b) Princess Anne or
    (c) Captain Mark Phillips?

15. Is the word **CHUKKA** used in
    (a) polo,
    (b) wild-west shows or
    (c) hunting?

16. Is **TIED-IN BELOW THE KNEE**
    (a) a fault in conformation,
    (b) a word used for hobbling a pony or
    (c) a kind of beauty treatment used on horses and ponies?

17. Is a **ROWEL**
    (a) a tool used for shoeing a horse,
    (b) a ring that is attached to a pelham or
    (c) a part of a spur?

18. Did **FELL PONIES** in the past
    (a) carry knights to battle,
    (b) carry lead from the mines to the sea or
    (c) pull stage coaches?

19. Is a **BROUGHAM**
    (a) a type of horse shoe,
    (b) a type of clipping or
    (c) a popular type of closed carriage?

20. Is a **LORINER**
    (a) a blacksmith,
    (b) a type of martingale or
    (c) someone who makes bits and stirrups?

Pony Club Show Jumping

Photographs by Findlay Davidson

The winning team from the Essex Hunt (South) branch. Left to right: Katrina Mason (13) on Maes Mawrs Bay Lady, Michelle Lewis (15) on The General Chip Perana Pine, Annette Lewis (13) on The General Chip Crown Court and Emma Brown (15) on Patrick St. John

Above
Janette Pitt (16) and Miss Ment, members of the South Oxfordshire Hunt (South) team that finished second

Above left
Bridget Lee (14) rode Redskin for the Albrighton Hunt team that finished third

Left
Annette Lewis (13), a member of the winning Essex Hunt (South) team, on The General Chip Crown Court

Many Moods

Photographs by Sally Anne Thompson

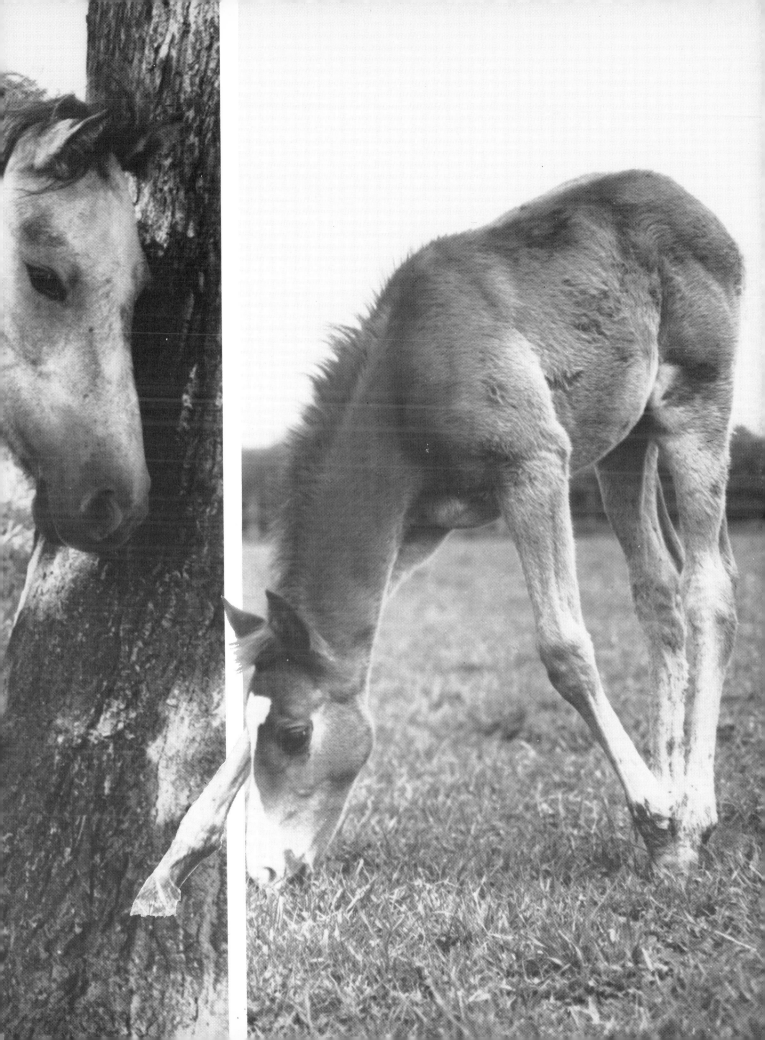

Dressage Has Its

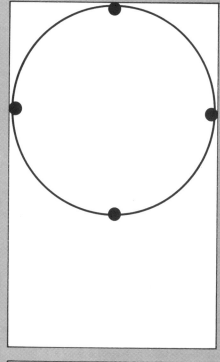

by Domini Lawrence

Dressage is often regarded as something to be got through as quickly as possible, before setting off on the important business of the cross country. In fact, however, the word means systematic gymnastic training to improve balance and paces, and should not be restricted to an occasional appearance in an arena.

Contrary to what many riders often feel, dressage tests do have their uses! They are designed to lead horse and rider from kindergarten to university and they provide both a target at which to aim, and a way to measure the success of your training. It is surprising how much more difficult it is to bring off a good transition when it has to be exactly at a marker, instead of whenever you happen to choose.

There are few perfect horses in the world. Most of them bend more easily to one side than the other, some are on the forehand, many lack impulsion. Dressage should improve these defects and accentuate the horse's good points.

The rider's job is to study the test at which he is aiming well in advance, and pick out the bits which may catch out his particular horse—and work on them. Once you have seen the traps, you are slightly less likely to fall into them! Equally, there will always be some movements at which, if all goes well, you should be able to count on picking up some extra marks.

If your horse is very obedient, but without brilliant paces, you should pull up on accuracy and straightness. If he has brilliant movement, that's a bonus, but soft, active transitions are even more important. Whatever your horse's talent, it is your job as rider not to throw marks away unnecessarily.

For instance, a circle should be round. And if you think this is too obvious a sentence, then a visit to almost any dressage competition will soon change your mind. Only too often, circles become egg-shaped!

When practising at home, four markers will quickly show you if you are an egg-merchant. Collect four bunches of dandelions—or

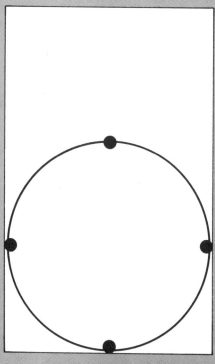

Uses

anything else easily seen—and place them as shown on one of the three diagrams below.

Then ride round the circle, just touching each marker, keeping the bend more with your legs than with your hands.

On a straight line, the horse should be straight. How difficult that is, but it does become a little easier if you think of keeping the horse channelled between leg and hand.

More marks are lost in transitions of pace than in anything else. This is, almost always, because the horse is not prepared *in time* for the next movement. As a very general rule, you need to be thinking one movement ahead of the one you are riding. This will help, too, with changes of direction, so that the change of bend is gentle rather than sudden or rough.

If the movements are ridden actively forward, and accurately, then the horse will become more supple and responsive, more balanced and attentive. He will be lighter and easier to ride, carrying himself and his rider with ease. Not only will he please the dressage judges, he will also delight his rider, and that is much more important!

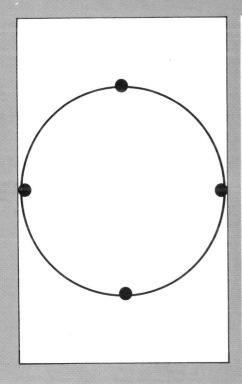

It is surprising how much more difficult it is to bring off a good transition when it has to be exactly at a marker

27

Fair Exchange

by Deborah Ghate

Illustrated by Carolyn Dinan

Choking back the tears, Helen scraped back her chair roughly

"It's no good," said Mr Oldfield, sympathetically, "you'll just have to accept it. Try to see it in a more adult light. After all, as soon as you sell him you'll be able to buy a new pony. A bigger one with more potential, more ability."

Despairingly, Helen tried to explain to her father yet again. "Don't you see? I can't sell Brambleberry. I just can't. He's served me faithfully all these years, and I can't just turn my back on him now. I love him. I wouldn't mind quite so much if I thought he'd have a good home; but Mike Talbot! Never!"

"It seems to me," said her father slowly, "that you are being extremely silly about this whole matter. You have completely outgrown Brambleberry now, and however much you love him, you cannot go on riding him for much longer; and I for one do not intend to go on keeping a pony that stands idle in a field all day. Either you sell Bramble now, whilst he is in relatively good condition, and buy a new pony with the proceeds, or you sell him and do without a pony. I don't care either way, but you'd better make up your mind quickly, I'm getting extremely fed up with this whole issue, and if you don't start being sensible, I shall sell Bramble with or without your permission."

Choking back the tears that would keep coming, Helen scraped back her chair roughly, knowing that her father disliked the noise, but not caring, she rushed out of the back door, slammed it shut, and ran down the garden.

"Oh dear!" said Mrs Oldfield. "I really don't see why you had to say that. It wasn't kind."

Mr Oldfield did not reply directly. Instead he said, "But the stupid child just will not listen to reason."

Down in the tack-shed Helen put on her riding boots and her hat, and collected Brambleberry's saddle and bridle. The tears, streaming down her face, fell in large, salty blobs that dropped heavily on to the clean saddle hanging over her arm, and ran down the flaps, taking the polish with them as they went. Brambleberry was standing clean and groomed in the paddock, waiting for Helen. When he saw her, he pricked his ears and let out a soft whicker of greeting. The tears fell faster.

The little black pony was impeccably groomed, and his whole stature suggested good health and excellent condition. Somewhere in his motley background there had been a Shetland pony, and so,

28

despite the mild spring weather, he had still retained his winter coat, which was jet black and glowed with marvellous lustre. Brambleberry had been Helen's first pony. He had seen her through her first bumbling efforts to ride, when she was nine, and now she was a confident fourteen-year-old rider. But her father had been right. The little 12.2 pony was now too small for her. He would have to go.

Quickly and efficiently Helen tacked up her pony. She let the stirrups down and swung lightly into the saddle. Gathering up her reins, she and Bramble moved off. Helen tried to forget the reason why she felt so miserable, and the morning was so fresh and sunny that she very nearly succeeded. But when they reached the top of the hill and she and Bramble stopped to admire the view, as they always did, it came swiftly back to her. She knew that when her father looked as determined as he had that morning, it meant that he had made a firm decision.

Helen dismounted, sat down on the soft, springy turf and let Bramble loose. He could be trusted not to leave her side. Sitting there, on the quiet hillside, she tried to sort out her tangled thoughts, but all that happened was that she burst into tears again. Getting up, she put her arms around Bramble's neck, and hugged him. "Oh, Bramble," she sobbed, "how can I sell you? I wish I could find you a good home, where I knew you'd be well looked after. Dad just doesn't understand. Maybe Mike Talbot *is* offering £230 for you and your tack. I know I wouldn't get that much for you anywhere else, but I know how he treats the ponies at his stables. I've seen him! When I first went there to try you over his jumps, I came away swearing that I'd never let you end up there, or anywhere like it, and I mean to keep that promise, no matter what Dad or anyone else says. You are not going there, *ever.*" And feeling better now that she had made up her mind, Helen remounted, and rode back home.

Helen dismounted, sat down on the soft, springy turf and let Bramble loose

The subject of Bramble's sale was studiously avoided for the rest of the day until the family was sitting in front of the television that evening. By this time Helen was feeling a lot calmer, and to tell the truth, she was beginning to feel slightly ashamed of her performance that morning. She felt that the best way to have dealt with her father would have been to stay calm and cool, and still flatly refuse to sell Bramble to 'that man', rather than to have rushed out in that melodramatic way.

Eventually she said, "Sorry about this morning, Dad. I didn't really mean to be so rude."

"You mean you've agreed to sell him to Mr Talbot?" said her father, sounding relieved.

"No-o," said Helen cautiously.

Her father sighed. "Well then," he said, "I've been thinking, and this is my final word on the subject. I'll give you until this time next week to sort something out for yourself. If you can find somebody who'll buy him for the same price, I'll tell Mr Talbot that he's sold. I can't give you longer than that, because he says he has another equally suitable pony waiting, if he doesn't know by then."

"I jolly well wish he'd buy it, then," thought Helen, but she said nothing.

That night, in bed, Helen lay making plans. "I suppose the best thing to do is to put an advertisement in the local paper or the village shop," she thought. Although she felt happier now, she knew at the bottom of her heart that it was extremely unlikely that anyone would pay £230 for Bramble, even with tack. He was really too small for a second pony, and even though he was exceptionally well-schooled, and could jump, gymkhana, and give a good display of collection at all paces, what first pony needed those qualities? All

Next morning Helen began to compose a suitable advert

the average first pony needs is to be quiet and well behaved. Unfortunately he was not good-looking enough for the show-ring and it was only because she was small for her age that she had been able to keep him for so long.

The following morning, after breakfast, Helen began to compose a suitable advert to put in the local paper. After an hour of deliberation, she came up with:

12.2 hh black gelding, 14 yrs. Make excellent first or second pony, quiet but very willing, jumps, gymkhanas, lovely ride. Good to box, shoe & catch.
Must be seen. Only for sale as owner outgrown. £230 with tack.
Tel. Flackford 24678

She then made out a card to be displayed in the Post Office win-

dow, using the same words as the newspaper advertisement but writing them in a variety of colours. After that she debated whether or not to ride to the Post Office and, in the end, decided that if she were going to lose Bramble soon she should spend as much time as possible with him. She would ride.

Trotting along the road with the advertisement and card tucked safely in her pocket, Helen's spirits began to rise. She decided to take a different route to the Post Office from her usual one, so she turned Bramble into Rose Lane and towards Flackford House, the local manor, which Helen had admired ever since she had been little. It was a rambling old house, surrounded by grounds of at least twenty-five acres, and the inhabitants of the house, a family called Tolworthy-Jones, were reputed to be very rich. All four of the Tolworthy-Jones children had ponies, and Helen had quite often seen them out riding, but they were always together and somehow did not make you feel that you could go and admire their ponies, and make friends with them.

At the end of Rose Lane a group of boys were playing about, and as Helen approached they began to giggle amongst themselves. Bramble drifted by happily until suddenly something came whizzing through the air, and hit him on the quarters. The little pony jumped violently, and when Helen turned round, she saw that the boys had catapults and were shooting stones. She urged Bramble into a trot, just as another stone hit her hat, and another her back. Suddenly a whole barrage of stones came flying at them, and Bramble, terrified out of his wits, began to bolt.

He galloped round the corner at full tilt, and Helen was completely unable to stop him. As he approached Flackford House, Bramble must have caught wind of the other ponies, for he swerved in through the front gate, which was unfortunately open, and galloped up the drive. But not until he swerved on to the lawn did Helen really begin to worry. "Oh no!" she thought. "All over their lovely, smooth, front lawn!"

But the worst of her worries were not over yet, for Bramble was now galloping along by some trees, and unfortunately for Helen, as he went underneath an old oak tree, a low branch caught her full in the stomach and swept her from the saddle. Just as she fell, the owners of the house came running out. A rather plump lady with a kindly face helped Helen, bruised and winded, from the ground.

"Oh dear . . ." began Helen. "I am very sorry . . .", but the lady said, "Now, now, don't you try to talk for the moment. You can explain later." And then, turning to the man with her, she went on, "Henry, the little pony will be all right in the paddock round the side, won't he?"

"I should think so," said the man, and took hold of Bramble's reins, for the minute Helen fell the pony had stopped galloping, and had been grazing calmly ever since.

Helen was ushered to the house and into a warm, comfortable room, where a fire was burning merrily in the grate. By the fire sat an old man in a wheel-chair. He looked very distinguished, with silver hair, and a fine silver moustache, and he was very tall. Addressing him, the lady said, "Now don't you talk to this young lady until she has had a chance to rest; she's just had a very nasty fall from her pony." She left the room and returned a few minutes later carrying a tea-tray with cups, plates and a big dish with an assortment of cakes and biscuits on it.

"Now then," said the lady, as she set down the tray, "are you feeling better, my dear? I'm Mrs Tolworthy-Jones and this is my father, Colonel Mountford." She turned round as the man who had looked after Bramble came into the room, then added, "And this is my husband."

Helen said, thank you, she was feeling a lot better, and then began to explain the reason for her presence on their property. When Mrs Tolworthy-Jones heard about the boys and their catapults she was very indignant, and said that something of the sort had happened to her when she was younger. After they had eaten their fill of cake, Mr Tolworthy-Jones suggested that Helen be shown round the grounds, and have a look at their ponies.

"I'm afraid all our children are away at school at the moment," he explained, "all our older children,

Suddenly a whole barrage of stones came flying at them

Duchess. I bought her a couple of weeks ago from a colleague of mine for Charlotte, but in the end we decided that she was too small, as she's only 13.2 and Charlotte's quite tall. It's a shame really as she's a beautiful animal." Turning to Anna, he said, "Go and fetch Perkins's headcollar and we'll bring him in. Then you can ride him round to the side paddock to see Helen's little pony."

Helen soon saw why Anna was able to make a ride out of going to the "side paddock"; it was quite a walk away. The little girl and her pony followed behind her father quite happily, showing herself to be a proficient little rider. On the way Mr Tolworthy-Jones fetched Bramble's tack from the tack room where he had left it, and after a short walk they reached the side paddock where Bramble was peacefully grazing. "Oh!" exclaimed Anna. "What a lovely little pony. What's his name?"

"Bramble," said Helen proudly. "Well, Brambleberry actually." And then after a pause, "You can have a ride on him if you'd like."

"Oh, Daddy, may I?" asked the little girl excitedly.

"Of course, if Helen says you can," said Mr Tolworthy-Jones, adding, with a twinkle in his eye, "providing he doesn't—er—bolt again."

"Oh, I'm sure he won't," said Helen quickly. "He's never done it before." She took the tack from Mr Tolworthy-Jones, and tacked up Bramble. As she moved round to the off-side of the pony to pull down the stirrup, she gave a little gasp. "No wonder he bolted," she said, pointing at Bramble's quarters. "Look!"

Mr Tolworthy-Jones and his daughter moved forward to see what it was. On Bramble's plump quarter there was a cut that had obviously been gouged out by one

that is. Our youngest daughter, Anna, is only five, so she lives at home."

Just as he said this, the door opened, and a small girl wearing jodhpurs and a black riding cap came in. "Hello, Daddy," she said. "Can we go riding now, please?"

"In a minute," said her father. "First I want you to meet Helen." After the introductions had been made, Mr Tolworthy-Jones took Helen and Anna outside. One by one the different ponies belonging to the various members of the family were pointed out to Helen; a Shetland belonging to Anna, named Perkins; a 12 hands grey, named Delilah, who belonged to the eight-year-old girl called Janet; a 14 hands dun called Sherbert, who belonged to 14-year-old Charlotte; and a 14.2 called Camberwell, who was the property of the

"Now then," said the lady, "are you feeling better, my dear?"

oldest child, a boy named Richard, who was 15. From the furthest corner of the field there appeared another pony, who galloped up to the fence where they were standing, while Helen stared with bated breath. She thought she had never seen anything so beautiful as this lovely creature.

The pony was bay, with a beautiful, bright and lustrous coat, and a thick, silky mane and tail. Its head was small and refined, with a proud carriage and slightly dished face that suggested an Arab background. Its pricked ears gave it a look of alertness and intelligence. Helen said quietly, "Who does it belong to? You didn't say."

"Oh yes!" said Mr Tolworthy-Jones. "This is Duchess. Dainty

of the stones that the boys had shot at him.

"Poor thing," said Mr Tolworthy-Jones. "That means that Anna must only have a very short ride."

Helen started to give Anna a leg-up, but smiling kindly, as though it was not really Helen's fault that she was so stupid, the little girl said she could manage and she proceeded to mount easily without any help. Helen then stood by the paddock railings holding Perkins, and watching with Mr Tolworthy-Jones while Anna trotted happily round the field. Soon Mr Tolworthy-Jones began asking questions about Bramble. How old was he? How high was he exactly? Who had schooled him? Just as Helen was answering this last question, Perkins chose to put his inquisitive nose into Helen's pocket, looking for the pony nuts that he could smell, and as he withdrew it he pulled out the card and envelope that Helen had prepared for the advertising of her pony. Mr

Tolworthy-Jones bent down to pick them up, laughing, but his face changed as he saw the wording of the brightly coloured card, which had fallen face upwards.

"I say," he said in a puzzled voice, "does this—er—relate to Brambleberry?"

"Yes," said Helen sadly. As she remembered where she had been going before Bramble bolted, and why she had been going there, the tears that she had managed to stop so far welled up again.

"My dear girl," said Mr Tolworthy-Jones, sympathetically, "don't be so upset." And then, quietly, "Tell me about it."

Helen began to tell him, glad to have someone to unburden herself on, and out came the whole story; Mike Talbot and her fears about him, her father's stubbornness, how she hated to lose her beloved pony, and her sadness at having to abandon him. Mr Tolworthy-Jones nodded solemnly at this narrative and then said gently, "I know how

you must feel about the Talbot fellow. I once took Anna for some riding lessons there, but I never took her back. The whole place was dirty and squalid, and the ponies tired and worn. I didn't want my daughter to ride in such a place."

As Helen burst into tears again, he added, "But don't despair, my dear, because I have a proposition to make. You say you don't think anyone else would pay £230 for Bramble, but I do."

Helen looked at him hopefully. "Do you really think so?" she asked.

"Yes I do," said Mr Tolworthy-Jones firmly. "In fact, what would you say if I offered to buy him for my little Anna? I think he would suit her admirably. He's quiet, reliable, gentle, and just the right size and temperament for her. He's had plenty of experience and he'd make the perfect replacement for Perkins, who's 23 years old now and due to retire. We would, of course, promise to give him a good home."

Helen lifted her head incredulously, but before she had a chance to speak Mr Tolworthy-Jones was talking again. "In fact," he was saying, "instead of using actual money, perhaps we could arrange a swop. Your Brambleberry for my Duchess."

Helen's thoughts drifted to the

Another pony galloped up to the fence where they were standing, while Helen stared with bated breath

She had just spent a lovely first day of the holidays.

beautiful bay mare. "But she's worth so much more than Bramble," she said.

"Well, perhaps in return you could have Perkins to stay in your paddock occasionally, or give Anna a few lessons on how to manage Bramble," said Mr Tolworthy-Jones. "I'd be happy if I knew Duchess had a good home." Helen could hardly believe her ears. To her it was all a dream.

She was still in that dream as she trotted home on Bramble, a letter in her pocket addressed to her parents explaining everything. When her father read the letter he was immensely relieved to find such a wonderful solution to the problem. Both he and his wife went round to Flackford House immediately, and they came back several hours later, saying what

nice people the Tolworthy-Joneses were, and with details of the exchange to explain to Helen. Bramble would go over to Flackford House as Anna's pony and he would live with all the other ponies there. Duchess would be sent over to Helen; and to make up for the difference in worth, Helen would give Anna some help with her riding every week. Helen was invited to go and use the riding facilities of Flackford House whenever she liked and also to meet the other children when they returned from school.

The following day Helen groomed Brambleberry thoroughly and rode him over to Flackford House. Anna and her parents rushed out to meet them and Mr Tolworthy-Jones took them round to the paddock where Bramble was

to live. Helen collected her new pony, Dainty Duchess, and prepared to ride her home.

"Well," said Mr Tolworthy-Jones, "how do you like her?"

"Oh," responded Helen, "she's simply lovely!"

"Fair exchange?" he grinned.

Many weeks later, Helen stood in the warm evening sun of spring. She had just spent a lovely first day of the holidays with her pony and the older Tolworthy-Jones children, who were now among the best of her friends. Her thoughts fell to Bramble, as they often did, and she thought of how her little pony had been so lucky. Anna thought the world of him, and he was very fond of her. Helen's thoughts then went back to Duchess, who stood peacefully grazing in the mellow sunshine, and to little Perkins who had, by his curiosity, enabled all of this to happen, and who was standing by Duchess's side, also grazing contentedly. He was paying a visit. Duchess lifted her neat and beautiful head and pricked her ears in her mistress's direction. She gave a gentle neigh and then resumed her grazing.

"Fair exchange," thought Helen. "Oh yes. Fair exchange!"

Buying a Pony

by Simone French

If, after months of persuasion, your parents finally agree to an equine addition to the family, or the pennies in the piggy-bank add up to the price of the pony you've always wanted, yes, it's a marvellous day.

A super, sunshine, pony-owning, fantastic day. But step down from cloud nine just for a moment.

Owning your own pony means a great many things. It will mean *commitment* on your part to taking care of it on a regular, daily basis—whatever the weather. It must be fed regularly at set times, checked over thoroughly each day and every piece of tack cleaned at least once a week. When the novelty wears off, will you still keep to this routine?

There are also the practical matters to consider. Keeping a pony requires the right *facilities*—for his sake. If he is to live out (and most ponies are happier out than in) he'll need some 3 acres of grazing in a safely-fenced field with shelter for bad weather and wet days. Can you find somewhere like this?

Then he'll need his own *wardrobe*. A saddle and bridle, of course;

The pony will need grazing in a safely fenced field

35

but he will also need water buckets, a manger, hay-net, grooming kit, blankets and bandages. Have you thought about these extra costs?

To keep all this gear safe you'll need *storage space*. You'll also need somewhere to keep his fodder. Hay, oats if you're feeding them, and bran. Will Dad let you have part of the garden shed, perhaps?

Next on the list is a sensible monthly *budget*. You must work out how much keeping your pony is going to cost. Include rent of the field, a monthly visit to the blacksmith, an allowance for veterinary charges (even if it is something as simple as rasping the pony's teeth or giving him a booster inoculation, the vet will always send in a bill), and then work out how much his feed is going to cost you.

It is false economy to buy anything less than top quality fodder. You'll either have to feed more if it's not of the best, or the pony will turn his delicate little nose up at it.

Find out how much hay, oats, bran, and nuts cost in your area and put all that down on the monthly account. Remember, you'll have to boost his daily ration of grass if you're working him hard in the summer, and he will definitely need extra feeds in winter when the grass is poor or non-existent.

Not daunted by all this?

Then let's get down to thinking about that pony.

Do get *expert help* in choosing him. If you're not a member of the local Pony Club branch, then join. Someone in that Pony Club will help. If you are not near a branch then contact The British Horse Society's County Chairman in the area (names and addresses for both the Pony Club and the BHS County Chairman can be had from The National Equestrian Centre in Warwickshire). You'll find that most horsey people are very happy to help. They enjoy

riding so much they want others to enjoy the sport too.

With that help, decide on the *type* of pony you want. Do you want an all-round pony? Or perhaps you want one that can jump well, so that you can compete—or maybe you're thinking of buying a pony to go hunting. Not every pony is good at everything. Search out one that is good at the things you want to do.

Next, you must consider *size*. It is dangerous to think of a big pony, say a 14.2 h.h., if you're a little person, or if you're thinking along the lines of ". . . I shall grow into him". Accidents happen when you can't control your pony. And nobody can control a pony that is too big for them.

But now you can ask your adviser to help *look* for the pony. If nothing has come up as a result of enquiries made to the local Pony Club branch, there are the 'For Sale' columns in *Horse and Hounds* and in *My Horse*. You can contact reputable dealers in the district or perhaps insert a 'Wanted' advertisement in some of the equestrian magazines or the local press.

When you think you've found something that sounds right, ask your adviser to go along and *try* him with you. Give the pony a good work-out. Beware a seller who, for example, is not happy to let you take the pony out on the road. Make sure he rides happily away from home.

Once you've found that dream pony don't, please, rush to take him home. Have him *vetted*.

Call in a veterinary surgeon you know. Tell him what you want the pony for. He will not only check the animal thoroughly for any sign of unsoundness or illness, but he will also assess the animal's condition and his suitability for you.

Then—at last—you can say, "That's my pony. I'll buy him."

That's when you climb back on to cloud nine. Happy riding!

The pony must be fed regularly at set times and checked over thoroughly each day

Crossword Puzzle

Answers on page 76

Down

1. Can be used on legs and tail (8)
2. For carrying strong drink when hunting (5)
3. A tree (3)
4. What the horse did with the oats (3)
5. Otherwise (4)
6. Some horses do this when they see a piece of paper (3)
7. Unhappy (3)
8. Started (5)
9. Lean forward when the going is . . . . (5)
10. Some horses and humans are afraid when it . . . . (8)
14. Used when studying horsemanship (5)
15. Remnants of the fire (3)
17. The horse's "point of elbow" (4)
19. Put on a performance (3)
20. To be won at the horse show (3)
21. Single (3)

Across

1. Where the bit rests (4)
2. The mare gave birth (6)
6. Formerly found on top of a show jump (4)
7. A bad fall might make you . . . . . (5)
8. Horses with black manes and tails (4)
9. The blacksmith will fit a new . . . of horse shoes (3)
11. More than 8 years old (4)
12. Use a slip . . . . to tie the pony up (4)
13. The breed from which the English thoroughbred originated (4)
15. An immeasurable period of time (4)
16. Racehorses like to feel this on their backs (3)
18. Used by the blacksmith (4)
20. Drawn by a team of four horses (5)
22. A single thing (4)
23. Come to pass by chance (6)
24. Your pony should know who's . . . . (4)

38

Pony Club Polo

by Cynthia Muir

Photographs by Mike Roberts

The stated object of the Pony Club Polo Tournament is "to interest members of the Pony Club in polo and to provide them with an introduction to the game and an understanding of basic principles, the rules and teamwork." How successfully this aim has been fulfilled can be seen by the ever-growing number of young players and the increasing list of top class performers whose careers began with the Pony Club.

The original suggestion that a Polo Tournament should be organized for the branches came from Colonel, now Brigadier, Barrie Wilson in 1958, and the first Tournament was staged in September the following year, with five teams taking part. The number rose to eight in 1960 and twenty teams now come forward to the Championships annually. There are now three Tournaments: the Jack Gannon Trophy, which is open to riders aged under 20, from mixed branches; the Frank Rendell Cup, a branch Tournament for riders under 18; and the Handley Cross Cup, a branch Tournament in which riders are 11 to 16. The two last-

The V.W.H. team that won the Jack Gannon Trophy in 1977. Left to right: Gordon Hunt (joint winner of the first Pony Club Polo Scholarship), David Yeoman, Jonathan Hanna and Robert Addie

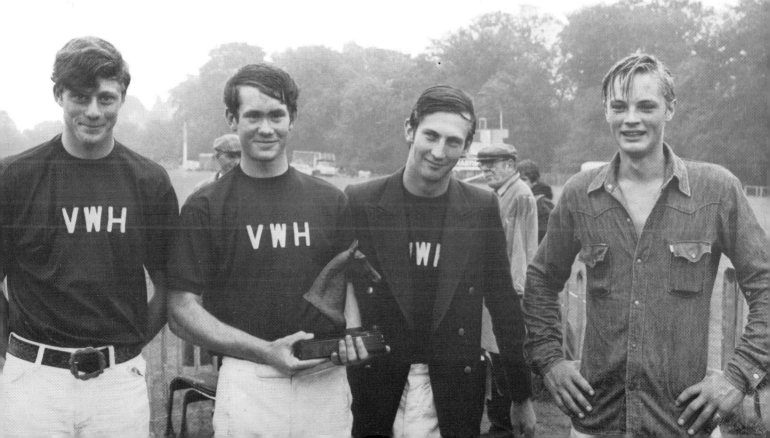

Robert Addie (centre) seen in action. His mother, Mrs Marjorie Williams, trains the V.W.H. Pony Club polo teams

named are the Senior and Junior Tournaments.

Regulations as to ponies for the three Tournaments differ; there is no restriction on the ponies for the Jack Gannon Trophy, but the team may not have more than eight; in the Frank Rendell Cup the team is limited to six ponies, which must not have been played in adult Medium or High Goal Tournaments or matches during the current year. Teams may have up to two spare animals in the Handley Cross Tournament, but the ponies, of any height, must have been ridden at rallies and must not have played regularly at official Adult Tournaments or matches. Girls form 20 per cent of the 100 or more Pony Club members who are now regular players.

The standard of play rises continually. A considerable improvement occurred when the hard ball became compulsory for Junior teams in 1970; Senior teams had used the hard ball for some time, as it was made compulsory for them in 1963. Prior to this a soft ball was used.

Polo's ruling body is the Hurlingham Polo Association, which has always given generous support to the Pony Club, helping it to stage training courses and Tournaments at different grounds. Lt.-Colonel Patrick Langford, a member of the Polo Committee since 1960 and the 1964-76 Chairman, has been an extremely keen supporter, and Mr "Buff" Crisp, from Kirtlington, the present Chairman, follows in this tradition and has sent display teams to

The standard of play rises continually. Girls form 20 per cent of the Pony Club members who are now regular players

visit Pony Club camps. A further fillip to Pony Club polo was given by Major Hugh Dawnay, who generously offered a scholarship, to be shared by two Pony Club players, at his Polo School in Waterford. The first winners were Gordon Hunt (V.W.H.) and Tim Verdon (New Forest) who had a week's course at the School in 1978.

The Championships change their venue every three or four years; recent sites have been Kirtlington, the Guards' Polo Club at Windsor and, in 1977 and 1978, Cowdray Park.

Among Britain's leading players who have reached the top via the Pony Club are Julian and Howard Hipwood, John and Eddie Horswell, Alan Kent and Sandy Harper. The Hipwoods, who are both 8-handicap, started their adult play with George Bathurst at Cirencester; both are regular members of the England team and also play a lot of polo abroad.

John Horswell, whose handicap is 5, started polo with the Pony Club when he was 15; after a year in the Argentine he joined Cirencester and was an England team member in 1976. His brother Eddie, handicap 3, won the "Best Young Player" Trophy in 1977. Alan Kent, now 24, learnt his polo with the New Forest Pony Club and, at 14, was the prizewinner at the Pony Club Tournament for "the player most likely to be a polo pony trainer," a competition judged by Colonel Guy Cubitt. With no ponies of his own, he has been lent animals, and was sponsored for two seasons by Mr Moller and, for the last two summers and this season, by a Nigerian. He has played in the Argentine, Australia, Dubai, France, Italy and the U.S.A.

Sandy Harper's handicap is 3 and his polo playing began before he became a Pony Club member; he played for Young England in 1972 and was the team's captain the next year. Olympic event rider, Hugh Thomas, played with the H.H. for several years. Young ex-Pony Club players now making their names include Oliver Ellis and Somerville Livingstone-Learmouth, each with a 3 handicap, and 16-year-old James Lucas, who already has a 1 handicap.

The winners of that first Pony Club Tournament in 1959 were the Hampshire Hunt branch; in 1962 came the first win by the V.W.H. and this branch holds a most remarkable record of success. When they won both the Senior and Junior Tournaments in 1977 they were recording their sixth success in each of the two categories.

The V.W.H. are trained by Mrs Marjorie Williams, who is herself a player. "Previously they were trained by Colonel Trevor Smail," she said. "His pupils included the Hipwood brothers and his own sons, Adam and J.P., who is always known as 'Jompy'. The Colonel played himself, and was a friend of Colonel Langford. Then, for a time, polo rather lapsed in the branch, but eight years ago (when my 10-year-old son, Robert Addie, was at Pony Club camp) I was asked to help in getting polo going again, and I agreed. There were very few players then, but we now have four teams."

There is now great interest among young riders in the Cirencester area, and several of the early members are still playing. The V.W.H. are allowed to play on Cirencester's stick and ball ground, and an annual Tournament there each August attracts 16 or 17 teams. Neighbouring polo-playing Pony Club branches include the Cotswold, initially trained by Mrs Williams, and the Bicester-Warden Hill. Mrs Williams receives considerable help from adult players, among them her husband, Jack, and Britain's top lady player, the 3-goal Claire Tomlinson, a daughter of Jack Lucas of Woolmers Park. Mrs Williams' husband spent many years in the Argentine, where he and his father bred polo ponies, and he is the equestrian adviser to the Sultan of Brunei. Robert Addie has become an extremely good commentator on the game and has had considerable experience at the Championships and in Brunei.

"My husband and I deal in polo ponies all over the world," said Mrs Williams. "A lot come from the Argentine, where so much polo is played, and there are so many ponies that there are always plenty of good ones to choose from. We get a good number of girls playing, and they are usually very brave, good riders and extremely keen. Children love polo, and it is very good for them, since they have to learn individual skills to teach their ponies to play as a team and to develop quick thinking and good riding. Just as Princess Anne's top-level participation has done a tremendous lot for eventing, so Prince Charles' example has helped polo."

Seven V.W.H. members played in 1977's all-conquering teams. In the Jack Gannon Trophy the team comprised Gordon Hunt, Robert Addie, Jonathan Hanna and Wylye Valley member, David Yeoman. Gordon is a farmer's son who has become a most successful trainer of ponies, and he now plays animals he has schooled himself. David and Robert spent last winter in the Argentine, trained by 7-goal Hector Barrantis, who lives at Trenque Lauquen, in Buenos Aires Province, and played with the "Mon Toto" Team, named after an Argentinian night club.

In the Frank Rendell Cup Team were Robert Addie, Tim Newman and New Forest members, Thomas Nelson and Caroline Broughton, and Tim was also in the Handley Cross Cup Team ("They are known as The Fluffies," remarked Mrs Williams) together with fellow members, Kate Cross, Rosemary Jane Barton and Ian Barr.

A backhander played by V.W.H. team member, David Yeoman, who spent a winter playing polo in the Argentine

Pony Club Mounted Games

Left

The winning Eglinton team. The riders were: Inez Noble, Fiona Farquhar, Debbie Moore, Peter Snodgrass and Frank Smith

Below

Sharpshooters' race. The riders are mounted bareback, two on each pony. They ride to the centre line where one rider from each pair dismounts and shies at targets until the heads are broken. The riders then remount and gallop back to the start

Above left

Flag race. Each rider gallops to the top of the arena and puts a flag in the holder. The rider then picks up a flag from the centre holder and hands it to the next team member

Left

Pyramid race. Each rider collects a carton from the top of the arena. A pyramid is then built section by section on a table

Caroline Bradley in action on the Countess of Inchcape's Berna, who was equal second in the 1977 Leading Show Jumper of the Year

Caroline Bradley

Caroline Bradley was born in 1946 and, though neither of her parents rode a great deal, both she and her sister had their own ponies at an early age. "We had four nice cheap ponies," said Caroline. "They all came from the same place and all of them were good. That's really how I became interested."

Most of Caroline's early instruction came through the Grafton branch of the Pony Club. She represented her branch in the Pony Club Horse Trials Championships on "a super pony called Just Jimmy". He was one of the four "nice cheap" ones, and he had been with the Bradleys since he was a yearling.

After gaining "A" levels in history and art, Caroline spent eighteen months at Lars Sederholm's Waterstock House Training Centre near Oxford, where she learnt a great deal about schooling horses. "Before I went to Lars, I'd take a horse out and trot it around and think I was doing some groundwork," she said. "But he made me think much more about it and try to work out what would suit each individual horse."

At the age of twenty, Caroline had her first overseas trip (to Dublin) as a member of the British team—and she celebrated this landmark by winning two classes on the Russian-bred Ivanovitch. Plenty of successes followed but, until 1977, when patient training with some of her younger mounts began to reap rich rewards, she was too often regarded as lacking the "killer instinct" needed to win big international classes. There were owners who took horses away from her just as they were ready to start some dramatic corner-cutting against the clock.

But all that has since changed. Caroline delighted three different owners when she finished first, second and fourth in the 1977 Basildon Bond Championship for the Leading Show Jumper of the Year at Wembley—and one of them, Donald Bannocks, had reason to be even more delighted the following spring when his young horse, Tigre, carried Caroline into individual fourth place in the World Championships and contributed to the British team victory. Everyone was delighted, since Caroline (who schools young horses through the winter, and seems to work about three times as hard as anyone else) was at last getting the rewards she so richly deserved.

45

John Bryan on his way to victory with Little Fleur, who was the leading horse of the 1978 point-to-point season

Riders of Renown

John Bryan

John Bryan, who was born in November 1959, learnt to ride almost as soon as he learnt to walk. He was taught by his father, who has a yard in Herefordshire to which owners send a variety of horses, among them point-to-pointers and show hunters.

As a junior, John 'had a go' at most branches of equestrian sport—including showing, show jumping, gymkhanas and hunter trials. He was a member of the Golden Valley branch of the Pony Club and was in their team for the Prince Philip Cup on several occasions.

He also took part in point-to-pointing when he was only fourteen and made a promising start by riding a young mare called Lucky Myth into third place. His first win came when he was fifteen on a horse called Jim Lad, who was also to carry him to his next two victories. Partly for this, and partly because he is "a lovely old horse and a super jumper", John regards Jim Lad as the favourite of all the horses he has ridden.

After the 1975 season, the *Horse and Hound Hunter Chasers and Point-to-Pointers Annual* said of Jim Lad: "Very game, and a fine jumper. Goes a good gallop, always looks a picture, and keeps on improving. Acts on any going but best suited by long courses. Very well ridden by J.R. Bryan."

There have been many other horses that have been very well ridden by John. He rode sixteen winners in 1976 and twenty-six the following year; on both occasions he was runner-up in the jockeys' championship to the experienced East Anglian rider, David Turner.

Then, having given everyone due warning that he was getting better and better, he ran away with the championship in 1978. In the process he created a new record by riding thirty-one winners, which represented two more than anyone had achieved before. It was all the more praiseworthy in view of the fact that he had broken his collar bone just two weeks before the 1978 season began.

John's other main interests are all connected with horses. He enjoys hunting, hunter trials and showing, but the most exciting part of his life occurs during those few months near the beginning of each year when the point-to-point season is in progress.

Chris Collins and Stephen's Society, the horse who turned to eventing after winning the Pardabice in Czechoslovakia

Chris Collins

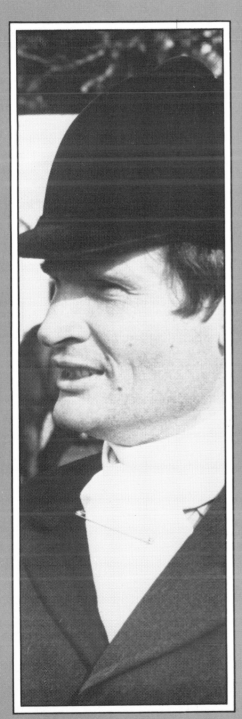

Chris Collins, who was born in 1940, is one of our few international riders who didn't find themselves on a pony almost as soon as they fell out of the cradle. He was twelve when a pony was lent to the Collins family and, as the eldest of five children, he may well have felt that he had proprietorial rights over it.

Having learnt to ride, Chris joined the Old Berkeley West branch of the Pony Club and, from then on, took part in all the activities that were held during the school holidays. "I was a very undistinguished member and was never chosen to ride in the Pony Club team," he said.

His sister, Anna (now Mrs Buxton) followed in his footsteps and she, too, eventually took up three-day eventing. But Chris's other two sisters and his brother, who rode as children, have since given up.

During the time he was at Eton, Chris went camping in Devon and had a day's outing at Newton Abbot races while he was there. This was to inspire him with enthusiasm for racing and, a few months after leaving school, he bought a horse at the Ascot Sales and began training him for point-to-points. From there he moved on to steeplechasing, was third in the 1965 Grand National on Mr Jones and won the Amateur Riders' Championship a year later. In 1965, he went to Czechoslovakia and won the Pardabice, which is widely regarded as the world's hairiest steeplechase, on Stephen's Society.

Chris's involvement in three-day eventing began after he had competed unsuccessfully in some hunter trials. "I was struck by how badly I rode considering all my racing experience," he said, "so I thought I would take up some other form of riding." With the help of Lars Sederholm (who trains both the rider and his horses) and with his own talents and dedication, Chris reached the top of the ladder in his new sport, though he found it much harder than he had anticipated.

He was tremendously lucky to gain such a super partner as the wonderful Irish-bred Smokey VI, who must have been just about the best cross-country horse in the world. Before his retirement at the age of fifteen, Smokey was placed at Badminton three times (1974, '76 and '77) and Chris was a member of the British team that won the 1977 European Championship, when Smokey finished in seventh place and was the only horse to complete the second phase with a zero penalty.

Ted Edgar riding Everest Lastic at Windsor. Ted was on the sidelines with an injured knee during 1978 after a fall with this horse at the Royal Show

Riders of Renown

Ted Edgar

Ted Edgar was born in 1936 and learnt to ride on the local blacksmith's mule. He was about ten at the time and he used to pass the blacksmith's forge on his way to school.

His father had been totally against him becoming involved with horses and ponies, but such was the young Ted's enthusiasm that a pony was eventually bought for him when he was eleven. A few years later he began riding show ponies, including one called Debutant that was bought for the Edgars by Glenda Spooner, from whom Ted received much helpful advice. In 1949 Ted rode Debutant to win the ridden pony championship at the Royal International Horse Show at White City.

Later he moved on to junior jumping with a pony called Tic Tac, who was bought with the help of Alan Oliver's father, Phil. The earlier resistance of Ted's father, Tom Edgar, had meanwhile been substituted by a real enthusiasm for jumping.

Ted himself was to become keenly involved in racing. He rode more than eighty winners in point-to-points, as well as six in steeplechasing, before he decided to give up the continuous battle with his weight and hang up his racing boots.

Naturally the show jumping continued. His first good partner in adult classes was a mare called Jane Summers, who had previously been saved from the knacker's yard. Some years later he acquired Jacapo, with whom he once completed the British Jumping Derby course at Hickstead with one arm in a sling. Jacapo was lent to David Broome for the 1974 Olympics and Ted married David's sister, Liz, at the end of the same year.

The grey ex-rodeo horse, Uncle Max, Ted remembers with particular affection. It was with him that he gained perhaps his most thrilling victory, when he won the King's Cup at Wembley in 1969. Most of his subsequent successes have been with horses sponsored by the Everest Double Glazing Company.

Ted hasn't received any formal instruction, but he has found people like Dick Stillwell and David Broome enormously helpful. He also reckons that hunting taught him a tremendous amount about jumping, and helped to speed up his reflexes.

Ted's other interest is his farm, which is partly arable while the rest provides grazing for his ewes and lambs. He says that farming gives him real pleasure, especially after the hectic travelling of the show circuit.

Derek Ricketts on Denham Hills, the horse with whom he won the Puissance at the 1978 Royal International Horse Show

Riders of Renown

Derek Ricketts

Derek Ricketts was born in 1949 and began riding at the age of three. He joined the Bicester and Warden Hill branch of the Pony Club and was later chosen to ride in some of their teams.

He was taught to ride by his parents and by the Pony Club instructors who helped his branch. He competed as a junior in jumping, showing, one-day events and gymkhanas.

Derek's father is a dealer, and it was with some of the horses in his yard that Derek moved on to adult jumping. One of his biggest thrills was winning the 1967 Foxhunter Championship at Wembley on a mare called Miranda. A couple of years later, when he was twenty, he had a phone call offering him the ride on a Grade C jumper called Beau Supreme.

The horse was then owned by Cecil Williams, who had jumped him himself until breaking a leg. The next rider had been sidelined with a broken ankle, so Derek became the third man to attempt taking the talented novice along the path towards international competition. The attempt proved highly successful and, in 1972, Derek was given his first chance to ride for Britain when he and Beau Supreme were chosen to compete in Ostend. They didn't win any classes there, but they jumped two clear rounds in the Nations Cup.

It was Beau Supreme who carried Derek to one of his most satisfying wins. That was at Dortmund in 1975 when he won the Grand Prix over a huge course.

Derek's best partner in recent years is the former three-day eventer Hydrophane Coldstream, who also came to him as a Grade C, and as the result of an unexpected telephone call. "Mr Ward rang me and asked me to ride Coldstream," said Derek, "as the horse had been having leg trouble three-day eventing. I was very impressed from the time I started jumping him. Our first show was at Heckfield, where he was placed in all his classes, then we went to Windsor the following week and won a section of the Grade C, before finishing third in the Novice Championship."

Derek, who used to go to Lars Sederholm occasionally for instruction, regards Hydrophane Coldstream as the best and most consistent horse he has ever ridden. He put up an admirable performance on Coldstream in the 1978 World Championships in Aachen, where he was a member of the winning British team. The rider clearly enjoys spending much of his life in the saddle, since his only other real interest is hunting.

53

Clarissa Strachan spends much of her time bringing on young horses. She is seen here schooling Radjel

Clarissa Strachan

Clarissa Strachan, who was born in 1953, was taught to ride by her mother who used to walk for miles across their Devonshire farm leading her on a small pony. Clarissa was also taught by her elder sister, Sally, who is six years her senior and went on to pass the difficult B.H.S.I. examination for instructors. She is now Mrs Bell-Knight and is living in Canada, where she and her husband event.

Between the ages of twelve and seventeen, Clarissa was in all the East Devon teams for the Pony Club Horse Trials Championships and she reached the final at Stoneleigh on one occasion. One of her best mounts was "a super pony called Dunameir", who went on to be a J.A. show jumper, and she competed on him at big shows all over the country, including Hickstead.

Clarissa also competed in show pony classes and in virtually every activity run by the Pony Club. She and Tony Newbery, who is much the same age, used to ride together in pair classes; they were also both members of the junior mounted games team that used to be run by the East Devon branch of the Pony Club.

At sixteen, Clarissa competed in her first adult horse trials with By George, and was lucky to do so since the minimum age had only just been reduced. Shortly afterwards, she became the second sixteen-year-old to win an adult event.

Clarissa's best horse is Merry Sovereign, who was bought from Ben Arthur in Cornwall as "a very hairy and muddy five-year-old." He was introduced to eventing in 1974 and proceeded to win two novice classes at the age of six. He was second at Punchestown in 1975 and fifth at Badminton the following year.

"He could have been second at Badminton in 1977," said Clarissa, "if I hadn't managed to fall off while he was jumping a clear round." She was still chosen for the team that won the 1977 European Championship, though her score didn't count, as Merry Sovereign had to be withdrawn before the show jumping phase.

That was a big disappointment to Clarissa, who had carried on after a refusal at the double coffin. "I was delighted to reach the finish of the cross-country," she said, "and I couldn't understand why everyone else looked so glum." She was unaware that her horse had a nasty gash across his chest.

Clarissa goes to Dick Stillwell for instruction about six times a year and she finds him enormously helpful. For relaxation, she visits her sister in Canada and rides the Bell-Knight horses instead of her own.

More Moods

Photographs by Jane Miller

Fergus

by Denise Amos

Illustrated by Elaine Roberts

"Fergus! Come on, Fergus!" The piercing yell interrupted my dreams. "Fergus, you lazy lump, don't just lie there!" I forced my eyes open and turned to look at her. The silly young fool was standing on the gate frantically waving a bucket and headcollar. If she thinks she's going riding at this time of day . . .

"Fergus, come here. It's Pony Club today!" She jumped down from the gate and came running towards me. "Come on, Fergus, Pony Club!"

Oh, my hooves and tail, I thought, not Pony Club! I don't like Pony Club. All that trotting and cantering around in circles, and sometimes even jumping! And

there's that dreadful mare, Snowflake, and fat Major Banks with the loud voice, who always tightens my girths.

"Fergus, you're a terrible pony." Ruth (she's my human) was standing a pony's length away. "Get up this minute!"

Nag, nag, nag, I thought. But still, she's nice to me, and I don't want to be sold, so I scrambled to my feet and ate the sugar she was offering.

"There's a good pony," said Ruth, buckling on my headcollar. "A big bucket of oats today, and you're going to see all your friends."

Hurrumph! Where did she get an idea like that? If that Snowflake comes anywhere near me I'll kick

her from here to Kingdom Come.

Two hours later I was ambling down the lane to Lymstead, groomed until I shone, and my bit tasting of metal polish. If I hadn't been going to Pony Club I might have felt quite smart, and picked my feet up a bit, but with that ordeal in front of me I was saving energy.

As it was, we had plenty of time to get to the rally field, and I arrived cool, collected and feeling rather pleased with myself. That is until I saw Snowflake, and Sylvia, her rider. They were showing off, doing half-passes all over the place, and most of the Pony Club was standing around, admiring them.

"Come on, Fergie, let's go and see everybody," said Ruth, trying to persuade me to trot over. I decided that a slow walk was much more dignified.

When we were quite close, Sylvia

saw us, and called out in a deliberately loud voice:—"Oh, hello, Ruth! You decided to risk coming, then? I gather his behaviour must have improved?" The cheek of the girl. There's nothing wrong with my behaviour.

"Oh yes," Ruth was saying, "he's a lot better now."

"I'll bet he is," said Sylvia, very sarcastically. Several other people and horses were giggling, Ruth was fidgeting with embarrassment,

and Snowflake was rocking on her horseshoes with laughter.

"I'll fix that mare," I thought suddenly. So I charged straight at her, swung round, and kicked out at her with both hind legs. Ruth fell off. Snowflake jumped back, just missing my hooves, lost her balance, and fell over me. I charged off down the field neighing with laughter. Snowflake and Sylvia biting the dust! It was the funniest thing I'd seen for ages.

After that little episode things got tougher. Sylvia remounted, covered in dust, I was caught, Ruth returned to the saddle, and we had to go around in a circle with Major Banks in the middle. After a bit he called us to the centre: "Ruth, how many times have I told you about these girths? Mind your leg." He lifted the saddle flap, and I took a deep breath.

"But, Major Banks, he always blows his stomach out," protested Ruth. "Yes, I do," I said to myself. "How would you like your belt done up this tight?"

"Walk him forward, he's holding his breath." Foiled! I had to walk forward, the girths went tight, and I got knocked on the hock for cow-kicking.

"Okay, take him back out. Right then, prepare to trot, rising trot, trot on." He made us walk, trot and canter around that circle for ages, until he decided to do some jumping.

Now jumping is something else I strongly object to. They stick a jump in the middle of a field, and expect you to jump it. Not go around it, which is quicker and safer, or even through it, which is much more fun, but OVER it. Why? What's the point? I see that if you should happen to get stuck in a field that has no gate then it is very useful to be able to jump out. But if the field has no gate, then how did you get inside in the first place? Unless you jumped, which was a very silly thing to do.

Anyway, we had to do some jumping. There were five jumps, at least three feet high, and with horrible distances in between. I went around them, through them, and very occasionally over them. Major Banks said I needed a lot of schooling, fewer oats and a standing martingale. I'll give him standing martingales!

Snowflake did one clear round,

So I kicked out at her with both hind legs

I went around them, through them, and occasionally over them

and gave me a very superior look. I made a few rude remarks about horses with no sense of balance, and asked her if she'd seen the state of Sylvia's jodhs. Major Banks said that their jumping was quite good, but Snowflake was overbending because of Sylvia's heavy hands. I made a rude remark about horses with no mouths. Snowflake was now looking quite crushed.

After another round of jumping (or demolishing) it was thankfully time to go home. I began to do this with a great deal of enthusiasm, by belting across the field and cannoning into the back of Snowflake as we went through the gate. The stupid mare let out a piercing squeal, leapt through the gate, and dear little Sylvia nearly fell off again.

"Ruth! Can't you keep that animal under control?" shouted Sylvia. "No, I don't suppose you can. You ought to put a red ribbon on his tail, he's vicious."

"He's not vicious!" exclaimed Ruth. "He's just excitable."

"Excitable, my foot! Did any of you see the cavalletti he broke? Major Banks was furious." She questioned the other people who were nearby. "That animal couldn't jump out of bed."

My poor little Ruth was very upset by all this, and I wasn't staying to be insulted, so I decided it was time to go. I stopped galloping when we reached the village store. There's nothing like an ice-cream for horse and rider after a hard morning's work. Unfortunately Ruth had become rather hysterical. She shouted at me.

"No, you're not having an ice-cream, you greedy stubborn mule. We're going home, and *now*. You're going to do what I want for once." I made my intentions a little clearer

by backing into the telephone box.

"Ooh, you're a horrible pony," Ruth screamed at me. "Do you know what I'm going to do? I'm going to sell you, and buy an obedient pony. Then I shan't be the laughing stock of the Pony Club any more." She walloped me across the backside with her crop.

I was so shocked about her threatening to sell me that I quite forgot to buck her off, which is what I usually do if she hits me. I knew she didn't mean it, but even so I decided to humour her, and set off down the lane towards home.

I think I had better say a bit more about my home. I live in the heart of Devon, in a valley nearly a mile out from a little village called Lymstead, and a very long way from any big town. The house which my humans live in is awfully old, Elizabethan they say, and it's very isolated. In the winter we often get cut off by snow, and when this happens I have to take Ruth down to the village to buy food.

I trotted away down the track

that leads to our house, feeling rather worried. It wasn't often that Ruth got cross with me. Maybe there are little faults in my behaviour. Perhaps it was that squashed cavalletti. Yes, that must be it. Next time I'll go around the cavalletti.

When we reached home Ruth was still very annoyed. She put me straight in the field, with no feed, and she hardly bothered to brush the sweat off my coat. Is that the way to treat a hot, tired and hungry pony? I rolled in the dust to cool myself down a bit. I like dirt, it's comfortable, but Ruth has this tiresome habit of grooming me, so I don't like to indulge myself very often.

After a while Ruth's mother came out to see me. She's a very nice human and always brings me something to eat. This time it was a large carrot. I scrunched it up in delight. It's nice to know that someone cares. She talked to me for a bit, and then got into her car and drove away down the track. I walked over to the trees, because the day was getting rather warm, and stood dozing in the shade. It really was very hot indeed, even for August. The sun was blazing down, and there wasn't a cloud in the sky. Hardly a living thing

And it was moving towards the house

"Go on, Fergus. Go to the village"

dared move, and the breathless silence was broken only by the buzzing of flies and the swishing of my tail. I was having a lovely dream, about a stable full of juicy orange carrots . . . I could almost smell them, and hear them crunching between my teeth . . . In fact I could hear a strange sound . . . A kind of crackling . . .

Suddenly the silence was shattered by a distant shriek. I raised my head to look, and saw that the sun had fallen onto the hill behind the house. No, that was silly, the sun was still in the sky. It must be what they called fire, burning the grass. It certainly looked very hot, and I didn't like it. And it was moving towards the house.

Then Ruth came pounding over the grass waving my bridle and yelling something about the Fire Brigade. She shoved my bit in, vaulted on my back and cantered me towards the fence. Is the girl mad? What's wrong with the gate? I'm not jumping that . . . But we were over before I had time to think, and galloping down the lane.

"Come on, Fergie, faster!" Ruth screamed in my ear. "All right, all right, I'm doing my best!" We swung round the sharp bend at the top of the hill, and suddenly there was something blue and horrible in front of me. I shied violently, jumped back, and Ruth fell off. Then I saw that the blue thing was only a paper bag. What a silly place to leave a bag.

Feeling rather sheepish, I waited for Ruth to get back on again. But she didn't. She was sitting on the ground, looking a very funny colour, with her arm all twisted around. After a bit she stood up, but I think her arm was hurting because she said, "Ouch", and sat down again quickly.

"Fergus, go down to the village, quickly!" I stood there looking at her. Was she getting on again or not? "I'm not standing around here all day!"

"Fergie, go on, NOW!" I went up to her and sniffed around to see if she had anything to eat.

"Oh, Fergus, you stupid pony, go away!" she wailed. Then she actually picked up a stone and threw it at me. I have never had anyone do that before.

"Go on, Fergus. Go to the village." She threw another stone at me. It hit me on the rump, and it hurt. That did it. I wasn't waiting around here all day being pelted with stones. Neither was I going back home with all that fire around. I couldn't get in anyway—the gate was shut. (Perhaps there is some point in jumping?) No, I was going down to the village shop, and perhaps old Mrs Bond would give me an ice-cream. So I turned on my heels and went.

The door of the little shop was open wide, and Mrs Bond was sitting behind the counter, doing her knitting. She's a bit deaf, so I neighed politely before I put both front feet inside the shop.

"Oh, Fergus, aren't you a naughty pony?" she said. "What are you doing? Where's Ruth? Do you want an ice-cream, then?" (She talks like that, always asking questions.) Then she gave me an ice-cream, and pushed me out of the shop.

"Ruth, Ruth! Where are you?" she called.

"Where's Ruth then?" she said to me. "You've thrown her off, haven't you? I'd better get our Sarah to take you back then, hadn't I?" She hobbled over to the door at the back of the shop and called Sarah down.

Sarah is Mrs Bond's granddaughter who lives with her in the summer. I don't like her very much, as she bosses me about, but after the ice-cream I raised no objection to her cantering back along the lane.

She made me do what she wanted, and it was horrible

At the top of the hill we saw Ruth, who was sitting just where I'd left her. Sarah saw her and the fire at the same time. She called out something to Ruth, and then I had to turn round and gallop all the way back to the village. When we reached the shop Sarah jumped off me, and ran inside, shouting at Mrs Bond. Then she went down the street banging on all the doors. Soon everybody was getting very excited and running around waving buckets and shouting, which was rather frightening. Then they all charged off down the lane.

After a bit Sarah appeared with a headcollar that wasn't mine, and smelt of another horse. She took off my bridle and put me in the field where the Pony Club had been. I was just calming down a bit when two enormous red lorries raced down the hill and down the lane to the house. They were followed by a smaller white van, and a blue and white car with a flashing light on top. They all made a horrible wailing noise, and I was scared of them.

Then everything went very quiet, and it got dark. I went to sleep in a corner of my new field.

The next day Sarah, and a lot of children, and some of the Pony Club people came to see me. They all fed me polo mints and sugar, and said how clever I was—I'd saved the day. It was all very nice, but I didn't really know what they meant.

After that Sarah started riding me every day. She made me do what she wanted, and it was horrible. I stayed with her for the rest of the summer. She took me to Pony Club Rallies, and even to a gymkhana. And she made me go over ALL the jumps. Major Banks said that I had improved a lot, and would be a lot easier for Ruth to handle when her collar bone had mended.

At the end of the summer Ruth came and rode me back home. I was glad, and now I do what she wants MOST of the time. Sarah never rides me any more, only Ruth, which is how I like it.

In fact, we're out for a ride together now, along by the stream at the end of the Common. Oh, that's a tasty looking bit of grass there, hint hint! What do you mean, behave yourself? It's jolly wet in that stream, you know, and I'll jolly well drop you in it if you start getting *too* bossy!

63

Fig. 1

Fig. 2

How to Draw

The Gallop

To my mind, one of the most beautiful sights to watch is a horse in full gallop, with its movements so flowing and free. Somehow the riderless horse galloping captures the eye more than a thoroughbred being urged on by a jockey in a final drive at the finish of a flat race.

The actual mechanics of the gallop can be captured best in a slow motion film that enables you to watch each step. It is a four-beat pace, whereas the slower canter is three-beat. In the canter, there are two moments when the horse has three feet on the ground, while the galloping horse has no more than two feet on the ground at any stage. There is also a moment of suspension, when all the horse's legs are tucked up under its body, not stretched out

Fig. 5

64

Fig. 3

Fig. 4

Horses

by Christine Bousfield

as all the old pictures and prints used to show before the days of photography.

The horse's body is carried long and low, and the head is stretched out. Each foreleg reaches out as far as possible to cover the maximum amount of ground in a fast gallop.

In **Fig. 1** the horse is on one leg and pushing forward until he is on his near fore and off hind (**Fig. 2**). The near hind then leaves the ground and the horse stretches out, with the near fore supporting all the weight as he swings on to the leading foreleg (**Fig. 3**). The off fore then supports the weight (**Fig. 4**). and the hindlegs start to come under the body (**Fig. 5**). The body weight swings on forward and the supporting leg comes off the ground (**Fig. 6**). The horse or pony is then suspended above the ground in full flight, with its legs tucked up under its body. It is a moment that is not too often painted by artists, but it has proved its existence through being caught by the camera.

After that the horse's near hind starts to come to earth (**Fig. 7**) and it takes up the weight again as he pushes forward and on into the same rhythm of footfalls. The gallop is the most exciting gait to watch as well as being the most exhilarating for the rider.

Fig. 6

Fig. 7

Into Novice One~day Events

by Anna Buxton

The step seems enormous. From the back of a horse of perhaps only 15 hands, the prospect of entering an official British Horse Society Novice One-Day Event seems alarming, even if you have represented your Pony Club at the Area Trials. In reality it is not such a giant stride, for any horse that performs well in Pony Club events will be sure to do so also in official horse trials.

From the year in which you are 14 until the end of the year in which you are 18 you may ride as a Junior, and are eligible for selection for the team which contests the Junior European Championships. Until you are 16 you may compete only in competitions confined to juniors, but from the age of 16 you may compete also in adult horse trials.

Once you have decided that you would like to ride in a B.H.S. event there are a number of preliminaries that have to be gone through. The first step is to become a member of the B.H.S. and the Combined Training Group, or the latter only if you are under 17. The horse must then be registered with the B.H.S., he must be five years old or more and he may not be smaller than 15 hands.

Once registration has been completed the B.H.S. sends the entry forms, the registration stamps for the horse, and the Omnibus Schedule in which the details of all the season's Horse Trials are set out. A stamp must be attached to each entry form you send, and it is very easy to forget them. There are also 'Priority' stamps, one for each month, which you stick on the entry form for the event that you most want to go to in that particular month.

You also have to remember to post the form at the correct time. There is a two-week period between the day when entries are first accepted and the ballot day, and entries close shortly afterwards. If the event is oversubscribed, and many are, especially in the early spring, the organisers decide how many of the entries received by the ballot day they can accept, giving preference to those with 'Priority' stamps, and return the rest. So, if the event is popular and you miss the ballot day, you have no chance of the entry being accepted. But not all events are oversubscribed, and many, particularly in the more remote areas, accept entries until they close.

Registering and entering may seem a daunting procedure but the effort required is worth it, for B.H.S. events are nearly all extremely well run, and the cross-country courses are built to a very high standard.

Once your entry has been accepted, and the competition is looming on the horizon, it is a good idea to read carefully the Combined Training Rules for Official Horse Trials (which the B.H.S. sends you with the Omnibus schedule), for there are many traps for the unwary. The Disciplinary Committee rule the sport with an iron hand and the penalties for stepping out of line are severe. I was once banned from competing in B.H.S. events for three months because, having been eliminated for three refusals at a cross-country fence, I persuaded my horse to jump it at the fourth attempt and carried on round the course. I thought the action was justified as the horse was scheduled to compete in an international Three-Day Event in Belgium the following week, but the Disciplinary Committee took a different view!

Diana Henderson, the former Miss Thorne, was runner-up at Badminton in 1967. She is seen here competing in the 1970 Pony Club Horse Trials Championships

As the competition approaches the horse must be tuned up with some long canter work, and one or two days before the event he must be given a pipe-opener to clear his wind.

If possible it is a great help to walk the course the day before the competition for if the place is unfamiliar, and the course twisty, it is almost essential to walk it twice, and there is not usually time on the day. For a big competition such as Badminton, the competitors may walk the course four or five times.

When you arrive on the ground on the day, the first move should be to get your number and check your times—or dispatch a willing helper or parent to do so for you.

For the dressage the horses must wear snaffle bridles (until they get to the level where the dressage test is of Elementary standard). Boots, bandages, martingales and whips are not permitted for the dressage and spurs are optional. Studs are a refinement that may not have come into Pony Club life, but there is no doubt that they help when it is slippery, and I think that studs in the front shoes are just as important as those in the back, which are more widely used. Riders usually wear white stocks and navy or black jackets, although tweed jackets in novice events are perfectly acceptable. The standard of turnout is high and nearly all the horses are plaited.

The amount of time that you need to ride the horse before the dressage is a matter of knowing the horse and of using your judgement. The safest approach is to leave enough time to enable you to work through a period of excessive freshness. Lungeing is often helpful if the horse is difficult to settle, but if he seems in a good frame of mind when you first take him out of the box, it is a good idea, after showing him the place, to put him back in and work him for only a short time before the test. Many horses perform better without too much preparation.

The Preliminary dressage tests 5 and 6 used in Novice One-Day Events are no more difficult than the Pony Club tests, but the judges are less indulgent. In a Pony Club test the judge may well be satisfied if the pony is barely on the bit, but to gain good marks in B.H.S. events the horse must be properly on the bit, he must be active, straight and obedient. Inaccuracy is also more heavily penalized.

The show jumping follows the dressage. The courses are now mostly built with standard B.S.J.A. fences and they are bigger than you would expect at a Pony Club event. The maximum height is 3 ft 9 in, but the courses vary considerably. The most difficult would be comparable to a Foxhunter course, and practice in B.S.J.A. show jumping competitions is invaluable. For this phase the riders keep on their dressage finery but the horses may be equipped with running martingales, and may be bitted and booted as the rider thinks fit.

For the cross-country riders wear jerseys and crash helmets just as they do in Pony Club events. Most horses have either boots or bandages to protect their legs, but bandaging is an expert job and many people think that the risk of damage from badly fitted

Elizabeth Boone, fourth at Badminton in 1978, was another of the competitors in the 1970 Pony Club Horse Trials Championships

69

bandages or from boots worn to such a degree that the pressure on the legs is uneven is greater than the risk of a bang to an unprotected leg.

I take out the front studs for the cross-country as I think it is safer. When I had a fall at Badminton in 1977 and my horse trod on me he left a lasting and very painful imprint of his studded hoof on my leg.

For novice One-Day Events there is no minimum weight, but for intermediate classes and for Three-Day Events the total weight of you, the saddle, and if necessary a lead-filled weight cloth, must be 11 stone 11 lbs or more.

The cross-country fences at B.H.S. events are more imposing than at many P.C. events. Kinlet, of course, is an exception, for the Pony Club course is usually more or less the same as the course for

the novice horse trials. The fences may be bigger but horses usually jump big straightforward fences well, and they are easier to ride at. In some respects novice courses are less tricky than those at Pony Club events where many of the competitors are riding seasoned and extremely clever ponies. Novice courses are designed to test young and inexperienced horses, but they still have their share of 'problem' fences—coffins, ditches, drops and water obstacles—which have to be ridden with discretion. Combinations are usually set with simple distances for the average horse so they may require thought if your mount is particularly small or short striding. This also applies to the show jumping.

In the Pony Club speed on the cross-country is hardly a factor, but in B.H.S. events it is vitally important. To do well you have to put up a good time on the cross-country, and to incur no time penalties you have to cut corners and maintain a good gallop. The ease with which the optimum time (the time for no penalties) is gained varies according to the terrain—where the course crosses flat open fields more competitors will finish within the time than when it twists through woods, or climbs steep hills.

So with a good mark in the dressage, a clear round in the show jumping and no penalties on the cross-country, you have won your first novice event. Be sure to turn up at the prize-giving, for the harsh penalty for not doing so—or for not detailing anyone else to collect your prize—is forfeiture of the prize money. You are also expected to exchange your cross-country jersey for your smart dressage turn-out.

Perhaps it is the first step towards a win at Badminton. Perhaps, at least, the success may encourage you to try your hand at a Three-Day Event, or you may be selected for the final Junior team trial.

For a Three-Day Event both horse and rider must be considerably fitter than for one-day horse trials. The dressage and show jumping are similar, although the dressage test may be more advanced, but on cross-country day the test is very different.

A much longer cross-country course is preceded by two sets of roads and tracks and a steeplechase of between one and two miles. For this you need two good watches—one preferably a stop watch—for progress on the roads and tracks must be carefully timed. The speed for the roads and tracks is 240 metres a minute, which on average is a fast trot. For most horses the speed for the steeplechase is virtually flat out, and riders in their first Three-Day Event often find it hard to appreciate just how fast this is. In my first ride at Tidworth I finished the steeplechase thinking I had gone brilliantly—at one point I had even taken a check, thinking I was going too fast—and could not possibly have incurred any penalties. I was soon deflated when I found that I had no less than 35; I had not realised how slow my horse's gallop was, and it was an expensive mistake to make.

So if there are a number of differences between the Pony Club Horse Trials and the serious adult contests, there are a far greater number of similarities. Both provide a testing ground for the same range of skills from both horse and rider, and they are essentially the same highly enjoyable and exciting, if demanding, sport.

Richard Walker, seen here competing in the 1966 Pony Club Championships on Pasha, took the same horse on to win at Badminton in 1969

1980 Competition

1

The Prizes

The top prize in both age groups (senior aged 13 to 16; juniors 12 and under) is a fortnight's holiday at a residential riding school, up to a cost of £100. For the runners-up there will be twenty prizes of £3 postal orders (ten in each section).

What you have to do

First look carefully at the photographs which show six different breeds. Your task is to name them. The photographs are numbered 1 to 6, so you simply have to write down the numbers, together with the names you think are correct (i.e. if you think photograph 1 is a Shetland, write: "1—Shetland" and so on).

Secondly, imagine you have been asked to buy a horse or pony for a rider who wants to start competing in Pony Club one-day events, but has no previous experience of this type of contest. Then study the list of points entitled "The Buyer's Guide" and decide which you consider the most important. You have to list them all in order of importance. For example, if you considered "Good action" the most important you would write "(1)C" and so on down to 6.

Lastly, write a limerick starting with the line: "A girl at our Pony Club camp." If there is a tie, the limerick will decide the outright winner.

The Rules

Entries close on 6th January 1980. They should be addressed to: Pony Club Annual Competition, Purnell Books, Berkshire House, Queen Street, Maidenhead, Berkshire, SL6 1NF. Be sure to state your name, age and address, and to enclose the coupon which you will find on page 77.

The judges' decision is final, and no correspondence will be entered into regarding this competition.

The Buyer's Guide

A A placid temperament
B Well schooled and obedient
C Good action
D Ability to jump big fences
E Courage
F Experience in one-day eventing

5

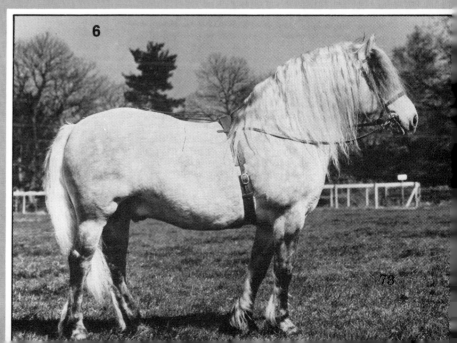

Pony Club Polo

Left

The Quorn team won the Handley Cross Cup for players under the age of 16. Left to right: Angus Shields, Hector Seavill and Nicholas Abraham

Right

The Final of the Frank Rendell Cup for players under the age of 18. The Berkeley/Cotswold team won by 2-0 from the Bicester

Tournament

Photographs by Mike Roberts

Left
The Berkeley/Cotswold team which won the Frank Rendell Cup. Left to right: Roger Allen, Caroline Worsley, Peter Trotter and Mark Baimbridge

Far left
The Jack Gannon Trophy, for players under 20 years of age, was won by the Cowdray team. Left to right: David Blunt, William Roberts, Alexander Mason and Nicky Evans

Right
Jonathan Abraham (Cottesmore/ Quorn) won the prize for "The Player to Show Most Promise" and Rosemary Jane Barton (V.W.H.) was "The Best Girl Player"

75

Readers' Poems

Memories

by Sarah King

Memories of the 'good old days' still linger in his mind,
He remembers well his mistress who was good to him and kind.
They often won a red rosette, attending the local show,
Once he had been proud and sleek, so many years ago.

His working days are over, his companions gone away,
Dear little chestnut Bobby and Snow-Cloud the friendly grey.
His paddock is bare and muddy – no shelter from the rain,
The poor horse gave up caring, he'd like a stable just the same.

No one comes to see him, he would love a kindly pat,
Or a haynet and an apple, something nice to make him fat.
Sad old lonely Dobbin, just left to slowly die,
No one to love and care for him, to find him dead and cry.

Dobbin

by Sarah Brookes

I have a little pony,
Dobbin is his name.
I know it's rather ordinary,
But he had it when he came.

His chestnut coat is shiny,
His eyes are golden brown.
And I feel proud to ride him,
In country or in town.

He may not be a stallion,
Nor a wonder horse.
But I think he's magnificent,
Because he's mine of course.

Contributions

The Editor will be pleased to consider any material (stories, poems, articles, puzzles, etc.) submitted for the next Pony Club Annual. Contributions, which must be the sender's own original work, should be sent to: The Editor, Pony Club Annual, Purnell Books, Berkshire House, Queen Street, Maidenhead, Berkshire, SL6 1NF. Please state your full name, age and address when submitting material—ages refer to the time when the material was written, not the date of publication. A fee will be paid for any contributions which are published in the Pony Club Annual. We regret that contributions cannot be ackowledged, but they will be kept until 6 January 1980, when the final selection will be made. Successful contributors will be notified as soon as possible after that date, and material which has not been selected will be returned to those who have enclosed a stamped addressed envelope for that purpose.

Readers' Quiz Solution

1 (b), 2 (a), 3 (b), 4 (b), 5 (c), 6 (c), 7 (b), 8 (a), 9 (c), 10 (b), 11 (a), 12 (b), 13 (a), 14 (b), 15 (a), 16 (a), 17 (c), 18 (b), 19 (c), 20 (c).

CROSSWORD

Across	Down
1. Bars	1. Bandages
2. Foaled	2. Flask
6. Slat	3. Oak
7. Shake	4. Ate
8. Bays	5. Else
9. Set	6. Shy
11. Aged	7. Sad
12. Knot	8. Began
13. Arab	9. Steep
15. Aeon	10. Thunders
16. Sun	14. Brain
18. Rasp	15. Ash
20. Coach	17. Ulna
22. Unit	19. Act
23. Happen	20. Cup
24. Boss	21. One

1979 Competion Results

The answers to the 1979 Competition were as follows:

Bridles and bits

1. Gag snaffle bridle
2. Snaffle bit
3. Eggbutt snaffle bit
4. Weymouth bit
5. Double bridle
6. Hackamore

Stable Requirements (judged by Lt.-Col. W.S.P. Lithgow, Executive Officer of the Pony Club)

1 (A) Good ventilation; 2 (D) Good drainage; 3 (C) No draughts; 4 (E) An interesting outlook; 5 (F) Electric lighting; 6 (B) A built-in manger.

The results were as follows:

Senior (aged 13 to 16). **Winner:** Christine Pattle (15), Juniper, Hillbury Road, Alderholt, Fordingbridge, Hants. SP6 3BQ. **Runners-up:** Anne Armstrong (14), Heddon Laws, East Heddon, Heddon-on-the-Wall, Newcastle-upon-Tyne NE15 0HE; Penny Davies (13), Andermatt, Granville Road, Great Harwood, Blackburn, Lancashire; Jackie Heron (13), Aeolian House, Morton Palms, Nr. Darlington; Helen McSweeney (13), 1480 Burg Street, Granville, Ohio 43023, U.S.A.; Jane Sawtell (15), 19 All Saints Way, Beachamwell, Swaffham, Norfolk; Elizabeth Crossland (15), Redminster House, Thurlstone, Sheffield S30 6RH; Joanna Wells (13), 5 Cobden Hill, Radlett, Herts. WD7 7JL; Karen Hope (16), 3 Cedarway, Whitehills Estate, Felling, Tyne & Wear, NE10 8LD; Amanda Driffill (13), Hazeldene, Ray Hall Lane, Great Barr, Birmingham B43 6JE; Susan Maria Holmes (16), 110 Moss Lane, Maghull, Merseyside, L31 9AQ.

Juniors (aged 12 and under). **Winner:** Zoe Walmsley (12), Treadaway House, Treadaway Road, Flackwell Heath, Buckinghamshire; **Runners-up:** Philippa Sansome (9), Little Chase, Kenilworth, Warwickshire; Leigh Edwards (9), Tan-y Banc Farm, Four Roads, Kidwelly, Dyffd; Julie Hendry (12), 1 Sunny Terrace, Vicarage Street, Painswick, Nr. Stroud, Glos.; Amanda Nalder (11), 2 Main Street, Stathern, Nr. Melton Mowbray, Leics.; Karen Tas (11), Moorhawes Farm, Sandhawes Hill, East Grinstead, Sussex; Samantha Payne (12), Wayside, Bridgwater Road, Lympsham, Near Weston-super-Mare, BS24 0BP; Wendy Bloor (10), Rhosmynach Fawr, Llys Dulas, Nr. Amlwch, Angelsey, Gwynedd, North Wales; Laura Shewen (11), Myrtle Farm, Bickenhall, Taunton, Somerset, TA3 6TS; Michelle Worthy (10), 3 Wyndham Road, Walkford, Christchurch, Dorset; Samantha Heath (10), Colley Irons, Shrewley Common, Warwick.